Advance Praise for *Rise to the Role*
by Randall Ian Thames

In an era where leadership is continually evolving, *Rise to the Role* serves as both a guide and a catalyst. Drawing from his transformative coaching experience at Korn Ferry, Thames presents the Discover, Develop, Display framework—a structured roadmap for leaders aiming to ascend with purpose and impact. The book is enriched with practical tools, insightful case studies, and leadership models that challenge conventional thinking. Central to Thames's approach is the principle of Decide: see the moment, honor it, master it, and rise to it. For anyone ready to lead with authenticity, elevate their influence, and leave a profound legacy, *Rise to the Role* is your definitive guide and unwavering companion toward true executive excellence.

−MICHAEL C. HYTER
President and CEO, The Executive Leadership Council
Board Director, Dine Brands Global Inc.
Author, *The Power of Choice*

Michael Hyter
President and CEO
The Executive Leadership Council

Rise to the Role

Randall Ian Thames

This publication is designed to provide accurate and authoritative information regarding the subject matter covered. It is sold with the understanding that the publisher is not engaged in rendering legal, accounting, or other professional services. If you require legal advice or other expert assistance, you should seek the services of a competent professional.

Design and cover art by Peaceful Profits.
Paperback ISBN: 978-1-967587-27-8
eBook ISBN: 978-1-967587-29-2

Disclaimer: The author makes no guarantees to the results you'll achieve by reading this book. All business requires risk and hard work. The results and client case studies presented in this book represent results achieved working directly with the author. Your results may vary when undertaking any new business venture or marketing strategy.

This book is dedicated to my family, friends, classmates, colleagues both professionally and in the ministry, the teams I've coached and everyone that I've counseled and mentored over the last 40 years. The poem, too, is a dedication to all because, as I tell my wife Trina and daughters Maya and Macy, deep inside you is a light that refuses to be kept inside of you. My hope and prayer is that this book inspires the insight that ignites the light.

The book is also dedicated to the moment. When reading this book, every reader needs to see their moment, honor their moment, and master their moment. When you master your moment, you begin a movement towards a monumental shift in your life.

Table of Contents

FOREWORD

In today's fast-paced, ever-evolving world, leadership is no longer just about achieving results—it's about inspiring transformation. It's about reshaping how we think, how we lead, and how we impact the people and communities around us. That's why *Rise to the Role* is not just timely, it's essential.

When I first encountered Randall Ian Thames' coaching and leadership philosophy, I was already a seasoned executive, tasked with growing and scaling a business and establishing authority in a competitive industry. But Randall's approach—rooted in his Discover, Develop, Display framework—challenged me to go deeper. His masterful blend of executive coaching, spiritual insight, and cognitive reframing helped elevate my leadership from effective to truly impactful. He helped me identify my unique individual gifts and traits and encouraged me to engage and lead from this core in order to lead differentially and, most importantly, authentically.

This book is a reflection of that journey. *Rise to the Role* is more than a guide—it's a blueprint for leaders and learners who aspire to inspire. Through witty case studies, practical leadership models, and a bold challenge to conventional thinking, Randall offers a fast track to unlocking your purpose, passion, and professional potential.

What sets this book apart is its architecture. Randall doesn't just tell you what leadership looks like—he builds a bridge to *why* it matters. He invites you to reframe your mindset, to lead with clarity and conviction, and to activate the leader within you. Whether you're leading a team, a company, or a community, this book equips you with the tools to rise—not just in role, but in impact.

Rise to the Role is a must-read for anyone ready to lead with purpose and leave a legacy. I'm honored to have experienced Randall's coaching firsthand, and I'm even more honored to introduce this powerful work to you.

John Starkey
President, Kimberly-Clark North America Family Care

Inspired insight ignites the light

Inspired insight ignites the light,
and leads down a path not seen through sight.

To your superpower it reveals the way:
The path to Discover, Develop, Display.

With God's spirit in us, the hard things ease,
revealing our true path and life's mysteries.

Your inevitable outcome is the ultimate goal
I know that you'll get there, well, happy, and whole.

Walk cheerfully over the world answering that of God in everyone.
–George Fox

Introduction

WHO ARE YOU NOW?

Every time the phone rang, I would drop whatever I was doing and run. I usually didn't have to run far because I spent almost the whole weekend hovering near it. It did ring—many times—but I didn't get the call. *That* call. The call from one of the coaches telling me I'd got into a team. I felt my life was over. I was eight years old.

Realizing my genuine distress, my parents stepped up. The following Sunday I took extra care deciding what to wear to church. I fidgeted all through the service and watched nervously when my parents approached John Sellers, who coached the Himyar Temple Little League team. He'd hardly looked at me at tryouts the previous weekend when I fumbled catches, struck out trying to bat, and threw a few pitches a three-legged kitten would be ashamed of. Sadly, he also didn't see me when I ran. Because I could run. Fast.

He didn't seem too enthusiastic, but it was hard to say no to two fellow parishioners, so he agreed to sign me up for the team, but—he told my parents—all the numbers had already been taken, except for Number 13. Even at the age of eight, I knew that symbols mean what you decide they mean, so I decided 13 was lucky. And for me, it was. Eventually.

At our first training session, it was obvious that most of the team had far more natural talent than me. But I realized that if I could take what was good in me and elevate that, I could create my own superpower.

My strong point was running, so I would go out and run on my own outside of official training times. I would play pitch and catch with a friend, or—if there was no one available—I would literally throw the ball up in the air and hit it. I would repeat and repeat and repeat. I was working hard to prove myself.

I spent most of that first year on the bench and then, toward the end of the season, the coach put me in to play. We were getting so badly beaten, he figured I couldn't make it worse. This was my moment. Finally, the skinny little kid with the thick glasses gets to step up to the plate, and—no, this isn't a Disney movie, and I didn't save the day—I struck out.

It was that embarrassing moment, and all those other embarrassing moments of being not good enough, being ordinary, even being less than ordinary that prompted me to say, "This is not what I want my life to be." I started to practice more. "I'm bringing out whatever I have," I decided. "I'm bringing it out, and I'm practicing, and I'm working on it, and I can do it on my own." I was pretty disciplined before, but this was next level. At the end of that year, my family moved to Hummelstown, Pennsylvania, and I joined another team, but I kept the Number 13, and I kept practicing. By the time I was ten, I was an all-star player.

Fitness is an important part of my life, and sports was the arena in which I learned to access my superpower through the discipline of practice and training, but it's just one aspect of being a fully rounded person. I am an ordained pastor and I have enjoyed a successful professional career working at prestigious firms, but my real focus is coaching. I advise executive leaders, boards, management teams, and committees to help develop organizational talent and strategies for success.

That's what the Inspirit process that you will learn in this book is about—using your inner talent, or superpower, to find your purpose and live your best life. It takes discipline and courage to take those first few steps on the path, but once you're in the rhythm of putting one foot in front of the other, the path leads—inevitably—to your desired outcome. It's at once very simple but also difficult and challenging, which is why I'm writing this book.

It's to help you every step of the way—to discover and develop your superpower, to help you overcome any obstacles on the path to your desired outcome, and to dedicate yourself to a life with purpose, a life in which you can have an impact and be seen to have an impact. Let's start where you are now—with who you are now.

WHO ARE YOU NOW?

Are you stuck in middle management when you know the C-suite is your natural habitat? Or are you just marking time in a rut, albeit a comfortable one? I often say the comfortable couch in life feels good but ultimately does not give you the support needed to keep you stable. Do you find yourself sliding two steps back for every one forward because the path you're on is steep and slippery?

Perhaps it's time to find a new path—the right path—to the outcome you desire. But you won't find it by looking up, down, left and right. You'll find it by looking within because you have what it takes to find that path, the path to your inevitable outcome. Each one of us has an inner talent or superpower that, when properly harnessed, can open up the right path. Once you're on that path, consciously and purposefully putting one foot in front of the other, it will lead to your inevitable outcome. I know that because I was lucky enough to discover my superpower and my path early on in life.

DISCOVER YOUR SUPERPOWER

I'd like to invite you to bring out your "inner winner" and harness your inner talent—your superpower—to make the world a better place. The great news is that we all have a superpower but it's meaningless unless we do something with it.

So, in this book, I'd like to help you discover your superpower, develop it, and display it—put it out there to help make the world a better place. Of course, it's unlikely that you will singlehandedly end world hunger, halt climate change, and bring about universal peace, but even making the world better for one person is an achievement of which to be proud. To paraphrase the Talmud, someone who saves a single life saves the whole world, so making the world better for one person can have a ripple effect that is incalculable.

In the same way that the flapping of a butterfly's wings in Florida can cause a storm in Hong Kong, your small, but definitely not insignificant, contribution can nudge another, which can nudge another, and—before you know it—there's a new normal. That's how every major change in history has happened. It took a few individuals speaking their truth about enslavement, mink coats, homophobia, witch burning, whale hunting, or child labor to slowly, but inevitably, change the dominant narrative.

But it's not just a matter of flipping a switch and watching it happen. Discovery takes curiosity and courage, development takes creativity and conviction, and display takes commitment and consistency. It's hard work. But you don't have to do it alone.

DEVELOP YOUR SUPERPOWER

Identifying your superpower is the first step, but, like in the biblical parable, just holding on to your talent is not enough. A talent buried in the ground—or buried within you—is of little value. You need to put it to work. As in the parable, that does involve some risk, but the rewards are immense. I went from the skinny kid sitting on the bench to an all-star player, and then to an executive coach and global speaker and motivator by developing my superpower. It took discipline, hard work, and—yes—a few knocks and a few tears. It will probably be the same for you. It will be hard work. It will stretch you, but it's only by developing your superpower that you will find your purpose and become the fully rounded person you were born to be.

DISPLAY YOUR SUPERPOWER TO THE WORLD

Your superpower is worthless until you work on it, develop it, and—ultimately—use it. So, it's time to rise and shine, to show the world who you are by displaying your superpower and using it to make the world a better place, to be a better person, a better player, a better friend, a better parent, sibling or child, a better employee, or a better boss. Show the world what you're made of, and let people see how the world is better because you are in it, exercising your superpower.

This book will take you step by step through the Inspirit process, which will guide you on a journey of discovery and adventure. You'll discover and develop your superpower, display and use it to make the world a better place.

That's what it's all about. Once you've identified, developed, and started using your superpower, the result is almost inevitable. You've consciously and purposefully set yourself on a course to success. That corner office is waiting for you.

TAKE THE FIRST STEP

Reading this book is a great starting point, but it can be so much more than just a quick read. It's a structured program, so it's most effectively read strategically, with purpose, and with discipline. Each chapter is designed to help you discover and evaluate aspects of yourself or the world, and each builds on the one before. Ideally, read it one chapter at a time, taking at least a few days in between to digest what you've read. Like the path it describes, it's a journey, not a destination. Savor it.

If you are ready to embark on an adventure that can transform your life from ordinary to extraordinary, read on. If you'd like a more personal touch, I do coaching for individuals, teams, groups, or corporations, and I'm available for speaking engagements. Feel free to contact me and my team at the Inspirit Institute (www.InspiritInstitute.com).

At the center of your being, you have the answer; you know who you are and you know what you want.
—Lao Tzu

PART 1

DISCOVER

When action flows from inspired insight, destiny is no longer a mystery—it becomes a masterpiece in motion.

The Discover phase is finding the materials required to build and support your base in life. Without the proper support, you are unable to elevate your plan and execute your purpose.

Chapter 1

LIVING WITHIN YOUR SUPERPOWER

It's your strengths, talents, and abilities that make you special.

When you are living within your superpower, you know you are exactly where you should be and are doing exactly what you should be doing. Once you get there, it can feel very easy because the path seems so clear and everything just opens up; but getting there may involve some hard work.

Some people naturally find themselves on a path that inevitably leads them to the outcomes they, consciously or unconsciously, desire. But most of us don't. Most people are stuck in ordinary mundane lives, careers, and relationships—unless they do something to change it, to become extraordinary.

When you connect with your superpower, your life is balanced, resting firmly on four strong pillars—physical, emotional, spiritual, and professional. Just like a house needs a strong foundation and a boat needs a rigid keel, achieving your inevitable outcome requires a strong central core. While the four strong pillars support your personal ecosystem, your superpower is a firm core around which you can move with graceful fluidity—like a martial artist with a core of steel who moves like water or a runner with flexible, relaxed arms and legs, flowing around a strong, straight spine.

Of course, you will need to focus on the professional pillar to get to the C-suite, but neglecting any of the other pillars will weaken the whole structure. We need all four pillars to support us as we move along the path to our inevitable outcome—the life we are meant to lead.

THE PHYSICAL PILLAR

Staying in the best possible shape is important for everyone, but for some people, it's their superpower. Take Jackie Chan, for example. He failed his first year in school, so his father sent him to drama school at age six. He soon realized that while he wasn't the brightest kid in the class, he was physically gifted, so he spent more time on his physical and martial arts training than the other school and drama subjects. And it's paid off. He is one of the best known martial artists and actors in the world and his movies have entertained millions—but at a cost. He is renowned for doing his own stunts, and he has had more than his fair share of accidents. His injuries over the years include a dislocated shoulder, broken sternum, cracked skull, crushed legs, dislocated hip, numerous spinal injuries, a broken cheekbone, and broken fingers. He's broken his nose four times, he nearly lost an eye after taking a high kick to the head, and he was in a coma for seven days. So, even if you are playing to your strengths and using your superpower, you may still face some serious challenges.

However, Jackie Chan has not neglected the other pillars. He has used his physical prowess to earn a very comfortable living for himself and to make the world better for other people. In addition to creating delightful movies, he's also contributed to animal rights and environmental causes and served as a UNICEF Goodwill Ambassador. He has bridged the gap between East and West probably more than anyone else, and among his many awards are stars on the Hollywood Walk of Fame and the Hong Kong Avenue of Stars.

It's not only athletes, martial artists, and action stars who need to strengthen the physical pillar though. The physical pillar focuses on how your health and wellness support everything that you do through your body and your movement. This is what allows you to keep up with the demands of daily life and to deal with where your body is taking you, with the natural attrition of that jar of clay, as I like to call it.

Maintaining your physical body—your jar of clay—is important because how you move and operate in your environment dictates how you live and whether you can be the master of your own environment. Mastering your environment means you have the strength to overcome the challenges of even the simple act of climbing a set of stairs. It's about keeping your physical body in the best possible shape so that you can perform at your best.

Harnessing your physical superpower can take you to new levels, personally, socially, and professionally, regardless of your starting level of physical performance. One of my clients decided at the age of 35 that she wanted to run a marathon. She had participated in 5K races before, but only as a walker. Still, she decided a marathon was what she wanted, and I was eager to help her reach her goal. First, we had to establish a strong mindset and then get her body to match her mind. It will come as no surprise that this took immense discipline on her part, but I was able to coach her through the progression of using her mental strength to strengthen her physical body. Through a series of physical challenges, she overcame discomfort and doubts and came to realize that each part of her body needed all the others to work in harmony to ultimately get her across the finish line. She completed her first (and so far, only) marathon in under four hours and came in ahead of me.

This physical achievement has had a significant impact on the other aspects of her life. It has helped her accelerate professionally because it taught her consistent discipline, and that ultimately translated to her obtaining a job she never thought she could have. Through this achievement, she gained the confidence to show up and perform on the job. She transferred the discipline of physical training to her job, and by constantly meeting and exceeding her Key Performance Indicators (KPIs), she created an opportunity for her inner light to shine. Soon after her marathon, she was promoted to an executive position in her existing company, which is kind of appropriate as she works for a large global health management organization.

THE PROFESSIONAL PILLAR

My client KS is the chief operating officer of a four-billion-dollar organization. Ten years ago, when he first consulted with me, he was a successful 40-year-old sales manager who felt stuck. Lost. He was making a good living doing something he was good at, but…there was something missing. After a few sessions with me, he came to realize that he was mentally stuck where he was, and he could not see his way out. He knew he had the business acumen and skills, but he was thinking like a sales manager, not a C-suite manager. I told him that he should not dress, talk, or work for the job he had, but to think and act like a senior executive—to elevate in place. While still at his old job he changed the way he spoke, swapped his casual gear for smarter clothes, and most importantly, thought like a CEO. I advised him to get out of his comfort zone and resign from his job. By changing the way he looked, spoke, and behaved, he had already created a path that would, inevitably, lead to success. But it wasn't a magic button. He left for a similar job at a smaller organization, and then he switched jobs two more times. It was a high risk move that paid off, and ten years after our first meeting, he is now the chief operating officer for a four-billion-dollar organization.

The professional pillar is about more than just clawing your way to the C-suite. It's how you contribute to your community, and it's what you do to make a difference for the people you serve—your customers, your employer, your audience, your clients, and your friends, family, and neighbors.

What you do is important because it's how you contribute to society, adding to the collective. You use your professional skills by directly creating something of value, or donating time or money, or creating opportunities for others to progress by creating employment. And of course, you contribute to your community by paying taxes or making direct donations to important causes.

A great example of someone with a business superpower is Apple founder Steve Jobs. Evidently, he was not the easiest person to work with, but most employees chose to stay even though they could have probably walked into other jobs with ease. That's because they recognized his genius in creating products that other people couldn't even conceive of and in showing the world that those products were indispensable. Consider that people who had never heard of an iPod or an iPad a year before all of a sudden couldn't live without one. Interestingly, he was motivated by love—not wishy-washy love, not love for people, but love for quality, innovation, and perfection. He trusted his own instincts and refused to bow to consumer pressure, believing that if he created a great product, people would line up around the block to buy it. And he was right. When someone suggested he do market research, Jobs famously quoted Henry Ford who reportedly said, "If I'd asked customers what they wanted, they would have told me, 'A faster horse!'"

Accessing your professional superpower is about faith—faith in yourself and your judgment—and dogged perseverance. It may seem a little counterintuitive to people on the outside, but if you are on the right path, you somehow just know, and you can find the strength to stay on it.

THE EMOTIONAL PILLAR

A beautiful (in every sense of the word) example of someone who had an emotional superpower was Diana Spencer, best known as Princess Di. Born into privilege and married into extreme privilege, she was more than just a glamorous fashion icon. She genuinely cared about people, and it showed in everything she did. Whether it was chatting to sick children or clearing minefields, she was motivated by genuine concern. Diana used the opportunities afforded by her privileged position to let her emotional superpower shine and to use it to make the world a better place. Kristen Stewart, who played Diana in the movie *Spencer*, did extensive research on her life in preparation for the part. Stewart said "Diana Spencer made people feel good" and that she had an "unstoppable light."

But it's not only fairytale-worthy princesses who have emotional superpowers. My client EU had had several jobs before she came to me for coaching. She was exceptionally talented and very good at her job, but she was a highly emotional person, which her employers saw as a hindrance because it made her seem less professional. Though her EQ was off the charts, it was unappreciated in the White, male-dominated world of financial and business consulting. So she suppressed it, and as a result, she was only giving a portion of what she could give. They could only see the work product and not the person behind the work, and that made her a limited asset. She was only evaluated for part of the value that she brought. So not surprisingly, she lost two jobs in a row, which is when she came to me for coaching.

The first thing I told her was:

> Don't ever let anyone tell you the value that you bring. If they don't appreciate your value, then create the job that suits you. Create a space in your existing job that will give you an opportunity to show them—yes, you're professional—but you're more than that.

I advised her to work to her strengths and let her personality shine. She did that. She moved to a company that appreciated her unique abilities and skipped two management levels. She was recognized not only for what she did but also for the beautiful person she was. During the coaching, we used the analogy of repotting a plant. Like a plant that's not thriving, she transplanted herself to a culture and environment that embraced her beyond just the work. She was able to grow because she was being nurtured in the ecosystem that was best for her. In moving from the harsh world of hard finance to the possibly more challenging, but certainly more caring, nonprofit environment, she found the perfect balance between her emotional strengths and her professional skills, and she moved from being a consultant to occupying a corner office.

Your emotional pillar is how you react and respond to situations personally, professionally, or in the community. When we react and respond based on our emotions, it creates a lens for people to see who we are. Importantly, I don't mean that we should always respond with emotion, but we should always have emotion in our response. We should always seek to respond with truth balanced with love. An environment with truth but no love is a hard environment that no one wants to be in, while an environment with love and no truth is a soft, uncertain environment that no one trusts. Neither of these feel safe.

THE SPIRITUAL PILLAR

A person renowned for his spiritual nature was Mahatma Gandhi. He was never a CEO but his influence on world history is immense. Best remembered for his nonviolent resistance to British imperialism in India, he was also influential in the anti-apartheid struggle. Martin Luther King Jr. was also strongly influenced and sustained by Gandhi's belief in the principles of *satyagraha*—nonviolent resistance. While a devout Hindu, Gandhi believed that all religions were equally true, and he worked hard to prevent the partition of the Indian subcontinent into Hindu India and Muslim Pakistan. When he needed to make a point, he often did it by fasting, and even when not fasting, he lived mostly on rice and water. His spirit was truly much stronger than his body, and those who tried to oppose him using violence and power were inevitably frustrated, because as Gilbert Murray wrote of him in a British newspaper in 1918:

> Persons in power should be very careful how they deal with a man who cares nothing for sensual pleasure, nothing for riches, nothing for comfort or praise or promotion, but is simply determined to do what he believes to be right. He is a dangerous and uncomfortable enemy—because his body, which you can always conquer, gives you so little purchase upon his soul.

Our spiritual pillar is the barometer by which we can live outside of our circumstances. We can live for something bigger and better. We can perceive our inner vision through our spirit. Spirit creates hope for us when life throws a curve ball. When we find ourselves in difficult circumstances that we don't like living through, the spirit brings strength. When our bodies start failing us, and our physical strength leaves us, it's our spirit that keeps us going. Some of the strongest people aren't defined by physical strength but have the spiritual fortitude to endure—and they understand that to overcome, you have to undergo. They see what really matters.

Without a firm spiritual pillar you can have no joy. Joy is about transcending your circumstances and living beyond short-term pleasure. A life in the spirit creates an opportunity for you to do that.

My client RT was a successful banking executive back in the 1970s when African American women like her were rarely seen in management positions in the banking sector—or any other sector for that matter. That's important. She was breaking barriers and shattering the glass ceiling in the banking world through hard work and dedication and consequently, creating opportunities for others to follow. However, while she worked hard at her career, her real passion was elsewhere. She was actively involved in her church and community, having served as a choir director, Sunday school teacher, and leader in the children's church, which she grew from just a handful of kids up to about a hundred students. She also became an ordained minister.

Despite her hard work and impressive progress at work, not everyone was comfortable having someone who looked like her in a management position. Things started going downhill when she was reassigned to another branch. The bank she'd been working in was a ten-minute drive from her home, but her new workplace was a one-and-a-half-hour drive. Each way. While some people may have considered her reassignment to be constructive dismissal, she used the commute to deepen her spiritual connection and to mentally prepare her Sunday lessons.

While she had support from some of her colleagues, there was continued resistance, but she persevered and found strength and courage in the growth she was experiencing working in the church. It was clear to her, though, that something needed to change. Together, we unpacked what was important to her, and we realized that leadership in the church was more important to her than leadership in the banking sector. It was growth and service that mattered to her, not professional recognition and financial reward. So when she was fired after two years of working at the new, distant branch, it was more of a breakthrough than a breaking point.

Rather than focusing on the fact that she had "failed" to progress at the bank, I advised her to focus on the immense successes she had achieved in the church. She did and five years after she'd been fired from the bank, she started a new church. Interestingly, she got a loan to build the church from the very bank from which she'd been fired, and many of the people who she'd worked with in the bank started attending her church.

The important thing here is that she didn't burn any bridges when she left. She took the challenge of working in a White male-dominated career and the disappointment of being fired and made it work for her. What the people who'd been trying to force her out saw was her spiritual superpower that showed through. The inevitable outcome was that everyone won because of her spirit.

It could be argued that she was just in the wrong job initially, but I don't think that is the case. Firstly, her breaking of race and gender barriers in the banking sector has opened doors for many African Americans and many women. And it's almost certainly her spiritual strength that enabled her to—using a biblical analogy she would appreciate—turn the other cheek. Her spiritual fortitude enabled her to persevere in a hostile environment, and working in the bank was an essential part of her growth. Without that experience, she would not have had the confidence, business acumen, and connections to start the church, to secure a loan for the church building, and to create a functional church that serves her community and satisfies her need for personal success and community service.

While her journey may appear filled with hardship, it was that collection of experiences that created the path to her natural outcome. It's almost as if she was lifting weights, and the pain of those difficult working conditions made her stronger, so she could attain her inevitable outcome.

Build a firm foundation for your life's journey.

Chapter 2

DISCOVER YOUR SUPERPOWER

Insight ignites intention; and from that spark, destiny is not discovered, but deliberately designed.

This chapter is about finding your superpower so that you can harness it to create the life you want. This may seem a bit weird, but it's where I start with all my clients. You need to gather all this information before you can create something of value. Think of it like baking a cake. First, you need to get all the ingredients together, and only then do you start mixing them, folding in the beaten egg white, and baking it at just the right temperature for just the right time. If you leave out any of these steps or get them wrong, you may still end up with something edible, but it won't be a delicious, beautifully light and fluffy cake. So before we start hunting for this hidden treasure, let's unpack the concept of a superpower.

It's your inner talent, and everyone has one. It's not restricted to people who are perceived to be high achievers, and it's certainly not restricted to people who can fly, walk on the ceiling, or see through brick walls. It's the special something you have that enables you to live better, get more done, and achieve an elevated status. But while everyone has a superpower, not everyone is aware of it or knows how to unlock it. Yours may already be wide awake, or it may be dormant, but every person has one. Everyone has that special something—that special star that shines within you, your special light. It's different for everyone, but it's that certain something that enables anyone to reach their full potential.

You'd think it would be easy to identify your superpower, but it isn't always obvious. There will be external signs that you're on the right path. For example, people may say, "Wow! That looks easy for you" or "How did you do that?" Another external sign is that you're getting paid to do things that are easy for you, and you get to see the impact of what you're doing. Those are all external signs, but they could be misleading, so it's just as important to pay attention to the internal signs. When you have the energy to work for hours at a time and you get lost in what you're doing, you can be pretty sure you're working with your superpower. You get so engrossed you forget to eat, and working gives you joy. When you tap into that superpower, you can achieve anything, so it's worth going through a bit of pain to find it.

AYANA MAKES IT HAPPEN

Ayana Parsons' superpower is the ability to see connections other people miss and to make things happen. She can see around corners, obviously not literally, but she has an uncanny ability to see potential that others may miss and to not be surprised by what less perceptive people may consider black swans. For example, take the Fearless Fund—the first venture capital firm built by women of color for women of color. When she started it in 2018, it seemed a pretty risky venture, but when George Floyd was murdered in 2020, it all made sense. Suddenly, it was cool and trendy to invest in Black fund managers. Obviously, she did not know this was going to happen, but her spidey sense gave her an inkling of the way the wind was blowing.

More importantly, though, she did not do it on her own. She was a catalyst. And perhaps, her real superpower is both being a catalyst and realizing that she can't do everything on her own. She used her superpower to bring about a dream team to make it all happen. Some were interns and one team member even worked every hour they could unpaid while continuing with their day job because they shared the dream—the dream Ayana portrayed so eloquently. They hustled and hopped to get that first $26 million dollars to kickstart the fund.

She had faith and she could kind of see the future, but the magnitude of Fearless Fund's success took her breath away. Interestingly, she feels immensely fulfilled by the fund's success, but more because of the bigger picture than because of how it reflects on her and the team. For Ayana, it's not about personal glory. It's important for her to have a positive impact on her environment.

She refuses the label of fame, opting instead for "greatness," because loosely quoting the great Martin Luther King Jr.,

"Greatness is determined by service," and everyone has the potential for greatness.

The concept of servant leadership also resonates with her because she has always been service oriented. Her mother was a social worker and education activist, so Ayana adopted the service mentality at the breakfast table, over family discussions, and through seeing how her mother would pour energy into other people. She was a positive light in the world.

Ayana tries to emulate her mother in everything she does, by manifesting light and being of service, and by being a servant leader. It's not an easy path, but it's a worthwhile one, and it's only possible because, as her mom advised, she does the hard things until the hard things become easy.

Repetition may make the hard things easy, but hard work is still the core around which Ayana has built her success. And that's one of the hardest lessons to learn when you are discovering, developing, and displaying your superpower. Yes, if you do the work, a successful outcome is inevitable, but it's not magic. You don't wave a Harry Potter wand and watch it all fall into place. It takes hard work. Lots of it. And regardless of what your superpower is, it needs to be backed by hard work and perseverance. And that's where Ayana really shines. As she told me in a recent conversation:

> Well, Randall, hard was what I did. I remember when I worked at Kimberly Clark, my boss told me, "Wow, you certainly are a hard worker." And it's true I really do work very hard, and as I pointed out to him, I'm also intelligent.

But a lot of people are intelligent, and I don't think that I have an outsized intelligence, but I do have an outsized work ethic. I don't think there's anyone who's going to outwork me. You might outsmart, but you're not going to outwork me.

This goes back years. I worked three jobs in college, doing whatever I had to do, because I had a vision, and I knew that I wanted to create a life for myself that wasn't going to come on its own.

It's that work ethic that enabled me to grind it out, year after year, knowing that I may get recognition, but I probably wouldn't. So that's why these accolades mean so much—and mean so little. I've got a whole wall of awards up in my office, which is great, but I don't do it for the accolades. Don't get me wrong, these are wonderful, but It's more important to me that I am making an impact. And that's my big achievement, I think. I can confidently say now, looking back, that I have left every single environment or organization better than it was when I started there. But I never did it alone, not once. I was just the catalyst.

It was this unique interplay between deep involvement and disciplined detachment that enabled Ayana to survive the impact of the 2025 injunction that prevented the Fearless Foundation from issuing grants to businesses owned by women of color. This struck at the very heart of the organization.

Speaking truth to power, she harnessed the discipline and determination that she's honed throughout her career, in both business and sports, and did not allow this to derail her from her inevitable outcome. Today she is a highly respected, very successful public speaker and advisor.

So, in short, Ayana has two superpowers: seeing around corners and catalyzing projects. But neither of these would be of any use without that Herculean work ethic. All the skill, talent, and genius won't get you anywhere if you don't get up off the couch.

SUPERPOWER, SCHMOOPER-POWER: AREN'T THESE JUST LEARNED SKILLS?

It's hard to nail down exactly what a superpower is because there is nothing superhuman about superpowers. Superpowers are everyday abilities that have been honed to a fine point. They're partly inherent because everyone is born with certain gifts and partly developed because the more you work on them, the more "super" they become. It's a mix of skills, talent, and discipline.

We all have talents, but they need to be activated. Sadly, though, some people with specific gifts and talents never express those talents because they stay in banal jobs and dull relationships out of a sense of duty, loyalty, fear, or a lack of ambition or energy. These are not necessarily bad jobs or abusive relationships, but they encourage a certain complacency, coasting along a gentle stream of a habituated comfort. All fine, really, but limiting.

It's a matter of curating, cultivating, and developing the superpower that is uniquely yours. But before you can develop it, you have to discover it, and that may be harder than you'd think. Most people have more than one talent, so it may not be obvious which of your talents is the superpower.

ASSESS YOURSELF

Discovering your superpower is a journey of self-discovery. It's a bit introspective, and you'll need to look deep within and ask yourself some powerful questions. So take a pause. Stop. Breathe.

Seriously. Stop. It is not easy, and you have to be authentic and honest with yourself. You may not be ready right now, and that's okay, but ask yourself why you're not ready. And then, gently see if you can persuade yourself to really, truly, honestly, and openly face these questions. If not today, maybe tomorrow. Maybe next week.

Now slowly and consciously answer the following questions. You don't have to write down the answers, but it helps if you do. So get a beautiful journal and start documenting your journey of self-discovery. It doesn't have to be beautiful, obviously, but it helps. Everything you do from here on is going to be the best, so your journal should be the best, too. It's like a treasure chest, a repository for your most precious thoughts and insights. It's special, so it should look special.

Are you sitting comfortably? Do you have your journal? And a sharpened pencil or a pen that works? Get ready for an inward and outward voyage of discovery.

Good. Let's start by looking inward to discover your deep, personal, subjective truth.

Slowly ponder and carefully answer the following questions:

- Who are you? Not what you do, but who you are.
- Why are you currently doing what you're doing?
- When was the last time you paused to question what you're doing and what you're contributing to life?
- What do you like doing when you're not getting paid to do it?
- How much time do you spend on special moments— either with friends and family or on your own?

Now that you've had that little introspective journey, let's look outward to get an objective perspective.

- How do you think other people—colleagues, friends, family, and even neighbors—see you?
- How accurate do you think your idea of other people's perceptions is?
- When was the last time you asked any of these people what they see when they see you?
- Did you like the answers? Why?

These answers create a foundation for an assessment—a starting point for your journey. While it's scary to learn how you're perceived by others, it's helpful to learn how you perceive yourself. This is how I work with my clients. I get them to look in, and then together we seek feedback from colleagues, friends, and family because it's important to know what others perceive your strengths to be.

So, following this pattern of moving rapidly from an interior perspective to exterior and back to interior, ask yourself and the people around you the following questions:

- When do you feel most comfortable and engaged—doing something you are passionate about and connecting with others?
- What are your most objective successes in life? What are the things other people are likely to praise you for?
- What abilities contributed to those achievements? What are the things other people believe got you there? (Spoiler alert—this is a big clue to your superpower.)
- What felt like it was absolutely effortless? That's another indicator of what your superpower is.
- What do people ask you for advice about? What do they consider you the expert in?

SPOILED FOR CHOICE: AB'S SUPERPOWER

One of my younger clients, AB, is very good at sports. As a child, she was always taller and faster than her peers, and she excelled at both lacrosse and basketball. Her physique, posture, and general deportment made it clear that she was an exceptional athlete, so the expectation was that she would play sports professionally. She went along with what the outside world was telling her. She was accessing an enormous gift and great skills, but it was not her real superpower.

I coached her in basketball and noticed that while it was clear she was very good and she was performing well, she didn't seem really happy or fulfilled. She loved being part of the team, and she enjoyed playing, but she didn't seem to have a real passion for the game. And of course, she enjoyed winning, but it didn't bring her real joy.

So I asked her, "What makes you happy?"

"I like the team," she replied. "I like playing."

It seemed her greatest joy in her success and victories was in the camaraderie she had with her team, but otherwise, she seemed almost indifferent. This conversation came at an important point in her career because college coaches had noticed her, and there was a good chance of her being offered a sports scholarship to a top college.

"You have to understand that this is the path that everyone sees for you," I said, "but is it the path that you see for yourself?"

For the next two years, as I was coaching her, I encouraged her to think about what interested her beyond sports. And, behold! She worked out that the thing she enjoyed most about playing sports was working with her teammates to solve problems, both on and off the field. In her senior year in high school, she said that she wanted to stop high-level competitive athletics and focus on what brought her joy—problem-solving. By focusing on her superpower, she was awarded an academic scholarship, which gave her the time and space to focus on her studies. She still played sports, of course, but only for fun and fitness. She graduated with a PhD in social anthropology, and she is working as a research analyst for a global consulting firm. By accessing her true superpower, she achieved superb academic results, landed a dream job, and is on track to become a partner where she'll soon have that office in the C-suite.

TAKE THE NEXT STEP

So having looked within, looked without, and asked other people, now put it all together. Consider the answers in your beautiful journal and see what they tell you. Is the picture becoming clear? Perhaps something is revealed that you hadn't considered for a long time. Whatever the results are, they are still premature. This is the very start of the journey. Think of your journal as a playbook, or a map book, that will ultimately help you find the way to your inevitable outcome.

The Discover phase of finding your superpower is checking that you have all the ingredients, or—more accurately—seeing what ingredients you have and using those to create the perfect metaphorical cake. By going through the self-assessment above, you have answered the question I posed at the beginning of this book. "Who are you now?"

So, who are you now? At this moment? Write the answer in your journal, preferably on its own page with a few flourishes. Maybe even add some color. You will be coming back to it.

Part 2, the Develop phase, is all about activating your superpower to elevate you to greater heights and set you on the path to the C-suite. It's a journey, not a destination, and I don't promise it will be easy, but it will be worthwhile. So get ready for a wild ride.

If you want to be a better leader, start by getting to know yourself. The more you understand what makes you tick, the better you'll be at managing challenges, building strong relationships, and leading with confidence.

PART 2

DEVELOP

Executive impact is a natural byproduct of executive influence, which is cultivated through a strong executive presence.

You've discovered your superpower, but that's just the beginning. It's time to develop it into a full-blown working superpower so that you can live your best life and elevate to the C-suite that is your inevitable outcome. If you're trying to choose between two or three potential superpowers, don't be dismayed. It simply means you are gifted in many ways, so it may take a bit more work to identify your superpower. Still, you can go ahead with developing it, because this process should help you home in on your true superpower. It may take effort and patience, but the result will be well worth it.

Chapter 3

TAP INTO YOUR SUPERPOWER

The light within is your greatest superpower. Let it shine unapologetically.

Having a superpower is of no value unless you use it. The most talented musicians, actors, and athletes are no better than the slobbiest of couch potatoes if they never get off the couch. The most important part of the path to your inevitable outcome is actually walking the path—putting one metaphorical foot in front of the other. It's not easy, and it can be frightening. While it's true that the path inevitably leads to your desired outcome when you are working with your superpower, it's not a straight and easy path. Like the biblical difficult path with a narrow gate, few take it, which is why so few people end up living their best life, whether it's in the C-suite, on the stage, in the arena, or just in life generally. But for those who do choose it, success is inevitable. Take, for example, one of the most successful business executives in the world—Richard Branson.

SCREW IT, LET'S DO IT: RICHARD BRANSON'S SUPERPOWER

As a child with dyslexia and ADHD, Branson did very poorly at school, and he struggled to fit in. Although he almost certainly didn't realize it at the time, his unique abilities were not so much a disability as a superpower. Famously, when he left school, his headmaster said he would end up either in prison or a millionaire. It turned out to be the latter because rather than focusing on what he could not do and lashing out at the world, he discovered his superpower, which had been hiding in plain sight since his childhood, and he utilized it for positive endeavors. (And that's probably a good thing because if he had turned to crime, he probably would have been a highly successful Bond-worthy evil genius.)

Dyslexia and ADHD were unheard of in the 1960s when Branson was at school, so neurodivergent children were simply labeled stupid, lazy, disruptive, or all of the above. Fortunately, we have come to realize that these are not inferior ways of seeing the world and processing information; they are simply different. A different way of perceiving and processing information is the basis of all creativity. So it is not surprising that some neurodivergent people become very successful. It's just a matter of how their abilities are perceived and used. Like many things, including knives and fire, they can be destructive or constructive, depending on the context and the way they are used. So, when Branson—almost certainly unconsciously—chose to use his unique perspective to change the dominant narrative about education in his first venture, *Student* magazine, he set himself on the path to his inevitable future. He used the magazine to further help ordinary people by offering records at discount prices. This led to the formation of Virgin Records, the success of which enabled him to branch out into railways, travel, health, telecoms, airlines, and—for Branson, the sky was not the limit—space. As predicted by his headmaster so many years ago, he could have wallowed in self-pity and allowed himself to be led into taking the easy route, possibly ending up in prison. But he chose the harder route, and he succeeded because he harnessed his superpower, even though it would be many decades before he realized that that was what he'd done.

Obviously, the 16-year-old Branson did not sit down and tell himself, "Dyslexia is not a disability, it's a superpower, so I will use it to become a multimillionaire." Using a phrase that has become one of the most-quoted pieces of advice ever, he just told himself, "Screw it, let's do it." He looked within, worked with what he had, and worked very hard and very deliberately to make the most with what he could do. And that, dear reader, is how you access and develop your superpower.

You have already taken the first step to understanding yourself by identifying your special talent—your superpower. Your main resources come from within. There are processes you use to activate your superpower, and these three principle external resources will support the process: people, places, and paraphernalia. Let's unpack them.

People

In theory, you could be like the Clint Eastwood character in Sergio Leone's spaghetti Westerns—a loner who needs no one and loves no one and just rides into the sunset when his job is done. But that's a lonely existence. Humans are social beings, and all businesses are only as good as the people running them and the relationships between these people. We need people at work, at home, and in our lives. Some are key stakeholders, some are important associates or friends, and some are more incidental. Think, for example, of all the people that a sports team depends on. The first and most important level is the players actually on the field. Without them, there would be no game. But the people on the bench are just as important, because while it looks like they're just sitting there, they are ready to step in for the players when they need them. And of course, the coaches and team managers are equally essential, as are the people cheering in the stands. We discovered how important they are in the early years of Covid. Many players reported struggling to find motivation when televised sports events were held without spectators in the stadium. There is something intangible about the presence of tens of thousands of supporters. They may not have the skills, talents, or abilities to work with you on the field, yet their support is invaluable. But it doesn't end there.

Think of the people who make the team's uniforms, the people who clean the locker rooms, the people who drive the bus, the people who ensure the players eat well, and the physiotherapists and other caregivers. It takes a village to win the Super Bowl.

To apply that to your journey to the C-suite, remember that every organization depends on many, many people. As you come up the ranks, you will meet and interact with many people—technicians, salespeople, cleaners, receptionists, and managers at every level. And the CEO who knows the name of the security guard at the door or the person in the mailroom is way ahead of the curve when it comes to making decisions that affect everyone and are critical for the success of the enterprise. As the successful playwright and entrepreneur Wilson Mizner so succinctly said, "Be nice to people on the way up because you'll meet them on the way down."

Get your journal out and list the people who are essential to your success, always bearing in mind that support is a two-way street. You can only depend on them if they can depend on you.

Places

You need a space or a special place where you can work on your process. It could be just a space in your mind, but there is a lot to be said for having a real, physical, geographical place where you can create what I call a mind gym, a place where you can mentally—or even physically—work out how you want to develop yourself. Many people think of the gym as a place to exercise their body, but there is also a mental gym where you can exercise your mind. It may be a personal space in your house, a chair on your deck, a shady spot in the garden, or even the actual gym. It's amazing how your mind can work when you do something repetitive and mechanical like swimming laps or running on a treadmill. My personal favorite is walking my dog, Nico, because we go outside into the woods where it is quiet and energizing.

There is immense power in silence and introspection, and there is a different but equally powerful inspiration that comes from being in the presence of excellence and intentionally surrounding yourself with how others express their gifts. I was in New York recently and went to the Whitney Museum of American Art. I was inspired both by the artistry—the aesthetic aspects of the exhibits—and the powerful narratives of how other people have discovered their best selves.

Another good choice is a concert. Watching a musical maestro or a prima ballerina displaying their superpower can be truly uplifting and inspiring, but don't dismiss the mundane. You can see people operating at their superpower in many different ways, places, and at every level. Take, for example, a building site. It's far from the C-suite but if you've ever watched construction workers throwing and catching bricks, you've witnessed true artistry. Without even looking at each other, one worker takes a brick from the pile and throws it up to the scaffold, and the other plucks it out of the air, gently puts it on another pile, and then turns around just in time to pluck the next brick from the air. It's like a dance, and every step of the dance is moving towards creating a firm, safe, and stable building. And a beautiful one, too, hopefully. Granted, this is a skill that is unlikely to get you to the C-suite, but it is a vivid illustration of working in the flow. So with that image in your mind, watch one of the top executives in your company doing a flawless board presentation. Like the construction workers, they never drop a brick.

Whatever place you've chosen for inspiration, you also need a space for execution. You need a space where you can be introspective and listen to your inner thoughts, your inner self. There is power in silence. There is power in the silence of listening to whatever is talking to you on the inside and stirring up emotions or ideas. If you need help in creating a space for yourself, turn to the people you defined in the previous section.

Paraphernalia

Almost every endeavor requires tools, and developing your superpower is no different. You need a way to make notes every time a brilliant idea strikes—even in the middle of the night—and to keep track of what you're doing. Some are obvious, like your phone, your laptop, or your journal. You'll also probably want a calendar—digital or paper—and perhaps a small notebook and pencil to write down those inspired midnight thoughts—your treasures. But out of sight is out of mind, so a great tool for keeping your inspiration top of mind is a vision board. It can be digital or analog, and it can be small enough to fit on a fridge or big enough to take up one whole wall of your home office. Digital vision boards are an option, but I believe analog to be better. There is something so tactile and intentional about cutting pictures out of magazines, placing them carefully in position, and gluing them onto a board. Sure, it does seem a bit like something you would do in kindergarten, but it works. It's an almost magical process of building your own world, exactly to your specifications. We'll deal with that more in the next chapter.

Additionally, a calendar can be more than a way of keeping track of appointments; it can be used as a suit of armor for your mental health and creativity. Blocking out an hour or so every day to be with yourself, to review your yesterday, and plan your tomorrow can save you more time than it uses up, and it can definitely reduce stress.

PROCESSES: PROTECT YOUR PEAK

It's time to activate your superpower by using your insights, actual or metaphorical space, and tools to create a series of habits, some of which are big picture but most of which are small, everyday routines. We'll start by identifying and listing your processes—your game plan or life map. But before you do that, you need to define the space in which you will execute these habits, and as any quantum physicist can tell you, space and time exist on an interdependent spectrum. There's no point having the perfect place to work if it's the wrong time, like when the kids are playing there or you have a carpenter putting up shelves. So timing is everything.

Not only do you need to ensure that the time you choose is right for your place, it also has to be right for you. If you are a night owl and always have been, don't be seduced into believing the hype that you get more work done between 5:00 and 7:00 a.m. than in the rest of the day. Sure, some people do, but some people don't, so if you're not an early morning rise-and-shiner, determine what your best time is. It may be just before lunch, in which case you will need to protect that time carefully by refusing to schedule meetings, take calls, or read emails. Granted, it's easier to impose this on colleagues if your peak time is early morning or late at night, but whenever your peak is, protect it. Possibly more important, disable all those pesky pop-ups. Regardless of their optimistic tone, they are not on your side.

This may seem selfish, but it isn't. Creating a cadence for yourself that enables you to have disciplined time is essential. You need your time to be open and free to do things that come into your head rather than following an externally imposed schedule or fulfilling the expectations of others. Because when you focus only on external validation, you leave no room for yourself to innovate and build up that internal treasure, the talent that's in you. This is not selfish because by being the best you can be, you are actually serving others. You're doing things for the job, for the company, for your family, for your friends, and for your pets. But you need to be very careful to first—consciously—focus on yourself because if you don't, you won't be able to serve others. Think, for example, how flight attendants emphasize that in an emergency, you must put on your own oxygen mask before assisting children or other people. That's because you need to be able to breathe to help someone else, and being selfless is of no value if you keel over halfway through trying to help someone else. It's hard, but you are of little use if you are burnt out and exhausted. You need to have the discipline to keep that time and space in place, maintain that cadence, and be consistent so that it's not just a one-off. It is *consistent* development that builds upon the foundation of the discovery of the talent that you have just unearthed.

PROCESSES: PERFECT YOUR PLAN

You have your place—your time and space—in which to work; you know who you can depend on—your people; you have all your tools—your paraphernalia; and you have a plan. But, as Benjamin Franklin is credited with saying, "If you fail to plan, you plan to fail." So perfect your plan by putting pen to paper or by opening a spreadsheet (but that isn't quite as delightfully alliterative).

It's not about how much you do and how busy you are. It's about being aware, tapping into something intentional, and being effective. Anybody can be busy, and many people are busy just because being busy makes them feel important. How often have you heard people "complain" about how overworked and busy they are, but you know they're really boasting. Well, they shouldn't, because busyness for its own sake is not effective. And people who live such busy lives that they don't have time to devote to their own well-being, their personal and professional growth, and their family and communities will burn out. I tell all my clients, "Let's get you effective and not just busy. And being effective means you are aware of the activities that you're doing."

So make a list of what you do every day to further your growth, but don't become so focused on, for example, business success that you neglect your family or your health. To ensure they stay balanced, I ask my clients to create an inventory of what they do every day for one week, divided into six foundations, which I call the six Fs because I love alliteration. They are field, faith, family, fitness, finances, and fun. Let's unpack them.

Field Foundation

Your field foundation is what you do. If you're a student, it's your field of study; if you're an athlete, it's your chosen sport; if you're a performer, it's the medium in which you perform; and if you are an aspiring CEO, it's your work—your occupation, your profession, your calling. The field section of your plan could include doing background reading about your company, designing a new and innovative process, finding new sources for procurement, or committing to arriving at work earlier and devoting your full attention to your work while you are there. So write down how many hours you spent on work and work-related tasks every day in your field column. This includes commuting.

Faith Foundation

Your faith foundation is easily overlooked, so you may need to pay particular attention to this one. For you this may entail regular attendance at church, mosque, or temple, but that is not the only way to feed your faith foundation. Being true to your faith may involve regular meditation, private prayer, reading holy texts, maintaining a commitment to doing good works or donating to charity, or even spending time alone with God, whatever or whoever you perceive that to be. So even if most of your faith commitments are on a Friday, Saturday, or Sunday, write down how many hours (or even minutes, they all add up) you spend on faith every day. If you don't belong to a specific faith community, you could spend some time exploring why that is the case, but do not feel pressured into joining a faith group if you don't want to. Living a good and moral life, being honest and truthful, and living consciously in the moment may be the foundation of your faith. And that's a good foundation.

Family Foundation

The family foundation is obvious, and it is one that is often neglected in the pursuit of professional progress. Whether you're the primary earner or one of several breadwinners, you work largely to support your family. So it is easy to tell yourself that everything you do, you do for them. Well, that doesn't cut it with a five-year-old. Children and spouses want time with their parents and partners often. If given the choice, they might opt for a smaller house and a skinnier bank account if it meant more quality time with the people they love.

Fitness Foundation

The fitness foundation is not only about jogging and going to the gym. That is a part of it, but it's also about eating well, getting enough sleep, brushing your teeth regularly, making sure you have regular checkups, and even driving safely. So when you write down how many hours a day you devote to fitness, be creative. Fitness refers to anything that relates to your physical health and well-being, and it is important because, quite honestly, you will not be an effective executive if you drop dead of a heart attack in the boardroom.

Finance Foundation

Your finance foundation is more than just working for a living. It's about saving, budgeting, and planning for the future and for unforeseen events. Except for time spent at the office, it's hard to measure how much time you spend on these every day because financial decisions and strategies are long-term. So you may need to do some mental gymnastics to assign it a time value. Start off by critically asking yourself whether you consciously create strategies to avoid putting yourself into financial discomfort. For example, do you have health insurance, household insurance, and a retirement plan? Those are positives, but they could be cancelled out by regular wasteful habits like taking a cab for two blocks instead of walking or regularly buying lunch instead of bringing a healthy homemade one.

Fun Foundation

Last, but absolutely not least, is your fun foundation. If you're not having fun in your life, you are definitely doing something wrong. Make time to do the things you enjoy, and it's okay if they overlap with the other foundations. Fun for you could be playing ball with your kids, in which case you can triple-dip with family and fitness, as can cooking a healthy meal for family—but only if you love cooking—and that's a quadruple dip because you can save money by cooking from scratch with fresh ingredients. It is okay to put off a bit of fun in the interests of getting things done, but don't overdo it. You can log almost anything you really enjoy as fun, but try to get at least half an hour a day just for you—read a book, go for a walk, watch a TV show or a sports event, paint, sculpt, or play the piano. It's a cliché but it's true that all work and no play makes you a dull person. Don't be a dull person; let your light shine.

After carefully recording how you spent your time for a week, you can calculate what percentage of your day you devote to developing each of the six foundations, on average. This will help you create a foundation from which to develop your superpower while ensuring you remain a happy, healthy, balanced human.

BALANCE OVER BURNOUT: CD SWITCHES SUPERPOWERS

Evaluating how well you balance the six foundational elements is essential to finding your niche. My client CD was an ambitious rising star who accelerated through the ranks to a high-powered executive position. Because she'd focused on her career, she had children in her late thirties, and in her mid-forties, she started questioning her priorities. She was progressing in her career, making money, and, apparently, successfully balancing a demanding job with raising two young children.

But she wasn't happy, and she found it hard to get through the day. She realized something needed to change, but she wasn't sure what. So I asked her to do a life evaluation based on the six Fs. CD found that she was accelerating in her profession but not in her life and that she was likely to burn out soon. She made protecting her peace her main priority. She left her high-powered executive position in a global transport and logistics company and used her executive superpower to execute an elegant sideways arabesque into starting and growing a very successful real estate company. She is still in C-suite management but not in such a high-profile position, and she still consults in business management. She has carefully and consciously gathered her professional and personal concerns together under the umbrella of protecting her peace, and she successfully balances great professional success with a relaxed and happy private life.

There's nothing supernatural about having a superpower. We all have one.

Chapter 4

TAME YOUR DRAGON

Fairy tales do not tell us dragons exist. We already know dragons exist. Fairy tales tell us the dragons can be tamed.
–Adapted from G.K. Chesterton

Having found and developed your superpower, you should be well on the way to your inevitable outcome, but there may be something standing in your way. Perhaps there is a metaphorical dragon greedily crouched upon the treasure of your superpower, blocking the way to your success. This is not uncommon, and while it may seem to be a problem, it may be an opportunity. This dragon may be another person who genuinely has it in for you, but it may also be internal.

Some of us are lucky enough to have lived a life free of major challenges and trauma. But most of us carry a greater or lesser load of negative baggage from our childhood, our recent past, or it may even be ancestral, and these can manifest as emotional issues that hold us back. Dragons. But that need not necessarily stop us from achieving great success in the corporate world. Take one of the most successful female executives ever.

TURN YOUR WOUNDS INTO WISDOM: OPRAH TAMES HER DRAGONS

Growing up in poverty and suffering multiple forms of abuse, Oprah was pregnant at 14 years old and suffered the added pain of losing her child soon after its birth. This was one of her biggest dragons and probably the first one she tamed. Oprah tried to hide the pregnancy, because like many rape survivors, she justifiably felt pain but also—quite needlessly—shame. When the story was leaked in 1990, she was traumatized and took to her bed for three days. However, having looked that dragon in the face, she recognized it for what it was. It wasn't a big, fierce, fire-breathing monster; it was a pathetic little lizard. As she wrote in 2007, "I soon realized that having the secret out was liberating," and that "holding the shame was the greatest burden of all."

One of the things that helped Oprah come to terms with her childhood was reading Maya Angelou's book, *I Know Why the Caged Bird Sings*. Angelou's childhood was similar to Oprah's, and she faced, tamed, and corralled similar dragons, as she described in her book. So having subdued the loathsome little lilac lizard of shame, Oprah harnessed it to help millions of other survivors of sexual violence and abuse in an ever-increasing and self-perpetuating campaign against gender violence. And her success is inspiring to millions of people who've suffered all kinds of abuse, hardship, and/or deprivation.

As a serial dragon tamer, Oprah has ridden them all, and they've all helped her move along the path to her inevitable destiny. She's been bucked off a few times and certainly suffered some nasty bruises and scrapes, but she's always dusted herself off and got right back in the saddle again.

She originally made her name as a talk show host, but she is so much more than a mega-successful entertainer. When she founded Harpo Productions in 1986, she was the first African American, and only the third woman, to own a major studio in the US. She went on to start Oxygen Media in 1998 and *O, The Oprah Magazine* in 2000. She was a billionaire before she was 50.

Oprah's dragons were—mostly—internal, but the world is not one big Oprah Winfrey fan club. She's also had to face some external dragons, like the ghastly green dragon of envy and the scaly, skinny dragon of fat shaming, and many of the malevolent manifestations of the dreadful dowdy dragons of discrimination, including the revolting red dragon of racism.

DRAGON BESTIARY

You may face many different kinds of dragons—some internal, some external, and some mythical. Most are internal, so perhaps your dragon is a long held belief that's holding you back, but it may also be a real live person who has it in for you. Many people have to face more than one dragon in their lifetime, but every person's dragon is unique, and they all have different styles of attack. Some of the more common types are listed in the following bestiary.

The type of dragon you face may depend on the type of person you are, on your background, or on where you are in your journey to the C-suite. All these dragons are focused on blocking your path to the treasure—your inevitable outcome.

The Ghastly Green Dragon of Envy

You need to be careful of this dragon because it attacks just when you think you are safe. It ignores you while you're struggling and striving, but once you've made progress, it tries to take it all away. This dragon is ambitious, avaricious, envious, and inevitably evil. Usually, it will try to take what you have, but if it can't get it, it will settle for harming you. Its natural habitat is the Planet of Small Pies, and it's difficult to tame because it believes, deep down, that it is in danger of starvation. This is because there is not enough food to go round on the Planet of Small Pies, and the dragons have to fight for every tiny morsel, which is silly because the beautiful behemoths of bounty on the planet next door simply baked bigger pies when they were faced with exactly the same situation.

While it's a difficult dragon to defeat, this dragon can easily be co-opted because it's not fueled by hatred or jealousy, but by fear. So the easiest way to tame it is to make creating opportunities for others an integral part of your journey to the C-suite. It's not a guaranteed strategy, but if you can convince the dragon that the pies on this planet are quite big, and that it can easily get a fair slice of that pie through hard work and dedication, it may change its nature completely. If you can't convince it, you may have to banish it back to the Planet of

Small Pies, where it can fight it out with its fellow ghastly green dragons.

The Disgusting Dull Dowdy Dragons of Discrimination

Most dragons, even if they are terrifying, are beautiful, but the disgusting dull dowdy dragons of discrimination are not. They are unable to appreciate the beauty and value of the world in all its diverse splendor, so they turn inwards and grow dowdy and dull. The many subspecies of this dreadful dragon include the horrible hairy dragon of homophobia, the zig-zag-striped xenosaur of xenophobia, the sleazy saurus of sexism, and the revolting red dragon of racism. In theory, these dragons have been banished from most workplaces, but they are insidious and many remain. Some have been merely swept under the rug from whence they emerge when least expected; some are hidden in plain sight but lightly disguised by corporate gobbledygook, doublespeak, and jargon; some of the more brazen ones hide behind the potted plants at the old boys' club, where they think they can't be seen.

All of these well-known subspecies can be particularly vocal, and even violent. They feed voraciously on ignorance, so they can usually be tamed by some light starvation and a change of diet. Sadly, none of the disgusting dull dowdy dragons of discrimination can be harnessed for any useful purposes, but once tamed, they usually find a comfy cave to sleep in and will hopefully stay there for a millennium or two.

The Loathsome Little Lilac Lizard of Shame

This particularly nasty dragon is a master of disguise. Appearing huge and invincible, it blocks your way to the

C-suite by entangling its unsightly, bloated body between the rungs of the corporate ladder, and it prevents you from speaking out by putting its huge, hideous claws across your mouth whenever you're about to speak up for yourself. This is the dreadful dragon that plagued Oprah for so many years until it was brought out into the light of day and was revealed as nothing but a pathetic little lizard. Once tamed, however, its pretty lilac hue and its sweet and beguiling voice can be harnessed to reassure you and others. It's a matter of getting it to start telling the truth. A particularly nasty subspecies of the loathsome little lilac lizard of shame, is the nasty, ugly, scaly, skinny dragon of fat-shaming, only evolved in the 20th century, so it's still refining its strategies and defining its true habitat. It subsists on victim blaming, crackpot wellness theories, outrageous fashion trends, and guilt. As with the loathsome little lilac lizard of shame, the most effective weapons against it are truth and compassion.

The Masked Imposter Syndrome Dragon

This is almost a back-to-front or upside-down dragon, as it perfectly embodies the childhood taunt, "liar, liar, pants on fire!" Whispering from behind its deceptive mask, it will tell you that you don't deserve the success you worked so hard for. As soon as you move one step up the corporate ladder, it will try to drag you down two, but it's a pathetic creature, so it will almost certainly need help from other dragons. Its most common allies are the yellow-bellied dragon of fear, the drab gray dragon of shyness, and many subspecies of the disgusting dull dowdy dragons of discrimination. The great thing about this dragon, though, is that it is easily neutralized once you've recognized it for what it is and have unmasked it. Like Zorro or the Lone Ranger, it's nothing without its mask.

The Ephemeral Invisible Dragon of Ignorance

While this dragon can be the most dangerous of all, it is easily tamed. Its natural habitat is the dark, where it is starved of all knowledge, but by its very nature, it is ephemeral and impermanent. By bringing it into the light and feeding it on good solid data, this dragon can be transformed into useful information and successfully ridden all the way to the C-suite. But, until properly tamed, it is very dangerous indeed.

The Drab Grey Dragon of Shyness

A master of camouflage, this dragon will create an almost invisible barrier behind which you can hide. When you're asked to do a presentation or take control of a project, it will find an excuse and step in front of you so that you can't be seen. And you won't be asked again. It's a bit of a gaslighting dragon that pretends it's protecting you, but it's not. By ostensibly shielding you from pain, it's preventing you from finding the path to the treasure that is your superpower and inevitable outcome. Taming this dragon requires great gentleness because it is easily spooked. You need to reassure it that you are strong and capable and that you are ready to step out into the world. But just in case you do actually need protecting, keep your dragon close to you, and let it grow along with you. As you grow in confidence, it will lose its drab grey coat and molt into a multicolored model of modesty that can protect you from the genuinely dangerous puffed-up purple dragon of pomposity.

The Puffed-Up Purple Dragon of Pomposity

This impressive looking dragon is not nearly as important or as prominent as it likes to think it is, and it often works in tandem with its sidekick, the big-headed, blinged-up dragon of conceit. Together these deceptive dragons disguise your true nature by hiding your faults and dismissing your limitations, thereby denying you the opportunity to improve your skills, make allowances for your weaknesses, and work to your real strengths. Fortunately, they are very vulnerable to reality checks. A hard look in the mirror has them quivering in their pointy-toed boots, and a well-placed prick from the sharp pin of reality will pop them, letting out all the hot air. Once they've fluttered to the ground completely deflated, they can be revived with a judicious application of mouth-to-mouth resuscitation. (Be *very* careful when giving mouth-to-mouth to dragons.) If carefully fed a diet of reality and truth, the newly revived dragons can be transformed into resolute reptiles of self-respect, be harnessed to the chariot of your ambition, and help to carry you to your inevitable outcome in executive management.

The Yellow-Bellied Dragon of Fear

This is a formidable dragon that usually manifests itself in one of two ways. It can wrap its powerful limbs around you and paralyze you so you can't move, or it can indiscriminately belch flame at anyone and everyone it sees, lashing out at both real and perceived threats. Neither of these strategies is particularly effective, and both are career-limiting moves. However, this is a great riding dragon. It's not easy, and you have to look it in the eye, put a strong bit in its fearsome mouth, saddle it, and mount up. Once in the saddle, with your hands firmly on the reins, you'll be able to ride it all the way into a corner office.

The Putrid, Pathetic Dragon of Poverty

This is a particularly pernicious dragon that can permeate every aspect of your life. Escaping it is difficult and requires both hard work and an element of luck. Sadly, though, it is pretty persistent, and you may find that even after you've escaped from its evil clutches—even once you're securely ensconced in upper or executive management—it refuses to leave you alone. It haunts your dreams, it whispers unfounded fears into your ears, and it can cripple you with anxiety. It's hard to tame, but it can be ridden to great advantage. It has an inherent fear of moving backward, so if you keep it contained, harnessed, and pointing in the right direction, it can help to drive you forward to your inevitable destiny by flatly refusing to return to its roots.

The Silly, Scarlet Saurus of Superficiality

This foolish creature is more interested in style than substance. It's all sizzle and no steak, or all icing and no cake. It's more interested in the perks of the C-suite—the corner office, the private washroom, the parking space, and the expense account—than in the work. Its bright color and pretty personality may blind stakeholders for a while, but ultimately, they will see through its sheer, insubstantial form and realize there's nothing there. It's a bit like the emperor with no clothes.

The Sleepy, Slimy Saurus of Sloth (and Its Morph, the Triple R)

This insidious saurus waits until you go to sleep and then lies across your body so that its weight prevents you from getting out of bed until way after your alarm has stopped ringing. And even when you're awake, it will slither around your legs whenever you try to take a step and wrap its slimy tail around your arms and hands whenever you try to work. One of the best ways of overcoming this dragon is to sit at your desk and open your laptop. It's scared of heights, so you will find less of them the further you climb up the corporate ladder, and it's also allergic to gym fumes.

Once properly trained, though, this sinister saurus can mutate into the remarkable relaxation reptile, or Triple R, which can be usefully harnessed at night to help you detox from your screen and slow down before bedtime. The Triple R really is a good dragon. It sleeps protectively across the foot of your bed to ensure you get a good night's sleep, it turns your alarm clock off on weekends, and it sneaks into your luggage when you're going on vacation. It's an unusual fire-retardant dragon that prevents burnout by ensuring you get the rest you need. It doesn't need much feeding, but it loves cuddles and long, leisurely walks.

The Comfortable, Cuddly Dragon of Complacency

This adorable dragon is prettily plump and apparently upholstered in comfy velvet fur. It finds a perfect place in the sun or shade (depending on the weather) to drape itself into a shape that is something between a couch, a hammock, and a well-sprung bed, and then it invites you to snuggle up. Once comfortably ensconced in its deceiving decadence, you can barely bring yourself to do anything. I mean, really, why bother when life is so good? This dragon will keep you in junior or middle management your whole life if you don't find the discipline to escape its delightful embrace.

The Pretty Pink, Problem-Pulverizing Dragon of Perfect Process

This incredibly useful dragon is happy roaming around in the garden, sniffing flowers, and nibbling on the grass to keep the lawn smooth until its services are required. It doesn't need extra feeding, but it does like to spend quality time with its human discussing world events, visualizing scenarios, and contemplating alternate futures. It's a very erudite dragon.

NOT SO TOUGH AFTER ALL

Don't be dismayed if you didn't recognize your dragon nemesis in the list above. Feel free to add your own dragon if you like because this list is not exhaustive. There are as many dragons out there as there are people because—spoiler alert—we create our own dragons in the same way that children create their own tailor-made monsters under the bed. That doesn't mean they're not real, just that they are only as real as you believe they are. As Terry Pratchett so eloquently illustrated in *The Colour of Magic*, dragons exist only if you believe in them. And that's the most important tool for taming dragons. You don't need a whip and a chair, or a magic shock collar, just the knowledge that the dragon exists only if you let it, and it can be whatever you want it to be. It can be a huge, vicious, fire-breathing monster; it can be a huge, powerful ally; and it can even be a small, reassuring talisman that fits in your pocket.

That may sound simple—and it is—but simple isn't always easy. Taming your dragon is not a straightforward, linear progression; it's a dance of give and take. There will be times when it seems your dragon has the upper hand and you believe it will always stand between you and your dreams, but it's when you access your superpower that its weaknesses are made manifest. So, rather than focusing on its weaknesses, focus on what you are best at. This works for actual external enemies as well, except that they don't always disappear in a puff of smoke when you find the courage to stand up to them. Awareness brings knowledge; knowledge brings purpose; and purpose brings us closer to our strength. Our strength creates clarity and self-knowledge, and that is what will weaken the dragon.

That doesn't mean that the dragon isn't real and that overcoming it won't be difficult, but it means that how you react to the dragon is more important than what, how big, or how powerful the dragon actually is. It is a tenet of Buddhism that you cannot control what happens to you, but you can control how you react to what happens to you, and that reaction determines whether the experience is good, bad, or neutral.

While it's true that most dragons are internal, some people face real, malicious, flesh-and-blood antagonists. I have a client who was faced with a real live nemesis in the form of the ghastly green dragon of envy.

PROCESS IS ARMOR: ECF NEUTRALIZES THE DRAGON

My client ECF is a second-time CEO of a nonprofit organization. He'd been in his role for three years when a new board chair was appointed. Even before he'd been appointed, the new chair made it clear that he did not have confidence in ECF. The first time the new board sat, the chairman started to challenge ECF's authority by telling the other board members that he was not qualified or competent to lead, disputing the bylaws and policies, and demanding that ECF deliver unnecessary reports and outcomes that had never before been required in that organization. Within months of becoming board chair, he formally petitioned for ECF's removal as CEO.

Realizing my client was under attack by a real external dragon, I told him the first thing we had to do was work out what kind of dragon it was. It took us a while but we eventually worked out that the chair actually wanted to be CEO himself, so perhaps it was the ghastly green dragon of envy. Interestingly, ECF's superpower is that he is a particularly charismatic leader, but I soon helped him realize that this particular dragon was immune to charisma. We needed something else. We needed strong, reliable, unimpeachable armor. So I advised ECF to stand on process and use it as his platform, his armor, his shield, and his weapon. It was time for the pretty pink dragon of perfect process to stop smelling the petunias and get to work.

With some help from me and the pretty pink dragon, ECF realized he could leverage his position as CEO by relying on accepted process and diligently applying the code of conduct in every interaction with the chair. Without calling the chair out on his actions, ECF complied with his requests by producing contracts when asked and supplying a meticulous inventory of anything related to his fiduciary responsibilities. He collated the organization's accounts, the meeting minutes, and reports from other executives. By carefully husbanding all these resources, ECF proved that he could balance his charismatic leadership with pragmatism and operational efficiency.

So when the letter calling for his dismissal was circulated, he had all the ammunition he needed to counteract the accusations against him. With his armor intact and his pink dragon at his side, he leveraged his charismatic superpower and met one-on-one with all the board members, the board liaison, and the other executives to deal with each of the issues that had been raised by the chair.

It wasn't just a defensive move, though. He used this opportunity to identify any areas of concern to discern how each stakeholder viewed him as a leader, and he learned what they believed his strengths and weaknesses were. He realized that he had been open to attack by the dragon because he had gaps in his defense and that he was not the fully rounded leader he could be. That's why he engaged me to help him develop as a leader, acknowledging that some aspects of his leadership style could be improved. Once he had ensured his armor was in place and that he had allies in the other board members and executive team, he carefully brought out his weapons, because this ghastly green dragon was not going to curl up and purr.

He presented verified information about the chair to the board, showing that he had sued three other organizations, had tried to unseat leaders in the past, had violated bylaws, and had generally been disruptive in previous roles. It was made clear that the case against ECF was unjustified. The chair resigned, and ECF and I are currently working on a plan to make sure that this charismatic leader continues to have an impact, inspire others, and help both himself and the organization move forward to better outcomes.

Sadly, the ghastly green dragon of envy proved to be unrideable, so rather than being tamed, it was gently neutralized and removed from the scene. As with the dragons in *Guards! Guards!*, the novel by Terry Pratchett, it is not dead, and it is not asleep. It's dormant.

Tamed and neutralized, but not eliminated and never defeated. Never underestimate a dragon. Never let your guard down.

Identify your dragon

- Why is it dangerous?
- How real is your dragon?
- What are its weak points?
- How can you tame it?
- Is it rideable?
- Describe in detail the armor you need, and list the weapons required to subdue, neutralize, or tame your dragon.

How can we forget those ancient myths that are at the beginning of all peoples, the myths about dragons that at the last moment turn into princesses. Perhaps all the dragons of our lives are princesses who are only waiting to see us once beautiful and brave. Perhaps everything terrible is, in its deepest being, something helpless that wants help from us.
—*Rainer Maria Rilke, Letters to a Young Poet*

Chapter 5

WALK THE PATH TO YOUR INEVITABLE OUTCOME

There is no path to your goal, the path is your goal.
—Paraphrased from the Buddha

You have identified and refined your superpower and effectively tamed or neutralized any dragons standing in your path, so now you are ready to walk the path to your inevitable outcome. It's not a straight path, and it's not an easy path, but it leads—inevitably—to your desired destination.

SOMETIMES SIDEWAYS, ALWAYS UP: INDRA NOOYI'S SUCCESS STORY

After joining PepsiCo in 1994, Indra Nooyi single-mindedly worked her way to the CEO's office. But it was not a straight trajectory. While keeping her eye firmly on the corporate ladder, she also changed companies or industries when it seemed appropriate—moving sideways to get a better shot at moving up.

Born in India, Nooyi completed a bachelor's degree in chemistry and a master's in business administration before taking the first step on her path to the C-suite. She worked as a business strategist for a British textile firm, and then as product manager for Johnson & Johnson, both in India. Realizing she needed to work in a broader arena, she moved to the US, where she obtained a master's degree in public and private management, working her way through college as a receptionist.

Her first job in the US was as a strategy consultant for the Boston Consulting Group. She then took a sideways and upward step to become Motorola's vice president and director of corporate strategy and planning. Her next upward and sideways step was to senior vice president of strategy, planning, and strategic marketing for the Zurich-based Asea Brown Boveri, where she stayed for four years.

In 1994, she took her final sideways step to PepsiCo as senior vice president for strategic planning. From then on, her trajectory was straight up. She was promoted to senior vice president for corporate strategy and development in 1996, and in 2000, she became senior vice president and chief financial officer, swiftly followed by another upward hop to become president and chief financial officer in 2001, when she was also given a seat on PepsiCo's board of directors. She was named CEO in 2006, and chair of the board a year later. She was the first woman of color and first immigrant to the US to lead a Fortune 500 company.

But while Nooyi was obviously focused on her career, she had a broader outlook. Her ever upward and onward career at PepsiCo was marked by significantly increased profits, a reduced carbon footprint, healthier products, and more equitable employment practices for the company.

From the outside, it looks like a seamless progression that just happened. And that's what this process is all about. Once you're walking in your superpower, you are on track to your inevitable outcome. But that does take planning. You need to stop and assess the situation before diving in. I call this the pause principle. It's similar to the way surgeons wash their hands before they operate. It's not just because it's a sanitary requirement, it also gives them a chance to mentally prepare. It's part of a ritual.

So, the first thing I do with my clients is a personal interview, during which we assess their current status by doing a SWOT analysis focusing on how they feel about their life and career and how they are perceived as leaders by their organizations.

ASSESS THE CURRENT SITUATION: SWOT ANALYSIS

The SWOT analysis is a structured way to assess your current state by evaluating your Strengths and Weaknesses and identifying Opportunities and Threats.

Strengths and Weaknesses

Your **strengths** will almost certainly include the superpower you identified in chapter 2, and they may be quite obvious.

Take, for example, my client MNO. She was an absolute wiz with numbers and accounts, and she had extensive experience in high-level financial management, which was obviously a strength, but she also had some **weaknesses**. As part of her upward trajectory, she was considering applying for a high-level finance position in a transport company, but she knew nothing about transport, so this was definitely a weakness. However, when creatively managed, a weakness can be an opportunity. As the great Chinese military strategist Sun Tzu said, "Victory comes from finding opportunities in problems." And that's exactly what MNO did.

Opportunities and Threats

MNO turned her weakness into an **opportunity** to learn something new and to show her potential employer that she was prepared to step out of her comfort zone—that she was a team player.

Threats may be your dragons—internal or external. External dragons could be people who want to block your path to success, but they are more likely to be competitors because you are almost certainly not the only person applying for a specific position or the only person working 14-hour days trying to get a foothold on the partnership ladder.

Internal dragons can be more dangerous, because they are insidious. There was a moment when MNO was in danger of falling prey to the ephemeral invisible dragon of ignorance, but she didn't. She tamed it by offering it a diet of information about the transport industry, and it turned into an opportunity she could ride all the way into her new position in that big transport company.

The good news is while there may be a dragon blocking the gateway, you may also find someone who can open it for you, or at least give it a nudge. This could be someone in your organization, someone in another organization, or someone not even in the industry. You may have a mentor who helps you in the same way that I help my clients strategize, construct game plans, and optimize opportunities. Mentors need not be permanent, and they need not even be formal. Anyone could help set or keep you on your path. It might even be the barista at your favorite coffee shop who mentions that someone is changing jobs, so you realize there is an opening in their firm. Or perhaps one of the salespeople might complain about a problem getting goods to the purchaser on time, which could give you an idea for a great opportunity to streamline deliveries, display your talent, and take one step further on that glittering path to your inevitable outcome.

Knowing that challenges often contain opportunities can help in stressful times. Like the classic hero's journey described by Joseph Campbell in *The Hero with a Thousand Faces*, things often seem to be at their worst when they are just about to become better. But it's not magic; you have to work at it. The hero does not miraculously elevate from rock bottom to their inevitable destiny. You have to claw your way out of the pit, inch by painful inch. You have to act, but even before acting, you have to visualize the desired outcome and every step you need to take to get there.

VISUALIZE YOUR SEQUENTIAL PATH

You know your desired destination, so now you need to plan your route. By deliberately visualizing your career step by step, the C-suite becomes your inevitable outcome. There are two dimensions to your path—a vertical one and a horizontal one—and it's more likely that you will follow a stepped trajectory with a few sideways shifts than an arrow-straight diagonal.

As a rule, your role will follow a vertical path as you climb the corporate ladder moving into positions of greater authority and status, but you also need to consider the horizontal aspect—whether you are working in the right company or even the right industry. So dream up some possible ways of reaching your goal with both upwards and sideways moves. Most importantly, when you dream, dream big. Reach for the moon, reach for the stars. Oh, whatever, reach for the sun! Seriously, dream big. Very big.

For example, if you're the ops manager of a small online retail company and you aim to be the CEO of a national airline, you will obviously need to gain managerial experience. But any experience in a company operating in or serving the aviation industry will stand you in good stead. So while looking out for any promotion in your existing company, you should also be actively seeking a position in a travel marketing, logistics, and/ or an aeronautics company. Or even a catering company that supplies an airline. The trick is to keep an open mind while keeping an eye out for mentors and allies. Ideally, you want to move into a position of greater authority as you change jobs, but it may be worth staying on the same level if you can move into a desirable industry or a more influential organization.

In the privacy of your own head, see yourself moving into your next position, either in the same company or in a different, more appropriate, or better one. See the slightly bigger office and list the perks in your head, but focus on the increased responsibility and the increased scope for making an impact. Now visualize every step you need to take to get there, and then turn it into a structured plan—a SMART plan.

MAP OUT A SMART PATH

Mapping out the path to your inevitable outcome requires setting sequential goals: SMART goals. SMART goals are Specific, Measurable, Achievable, Relevant, and Time-bound. Sequential goals follow on from each other, creating a solid base from which to elevate. If you are not yet in the right role in the right company in the right industry, you may need to plan your path carefully, concentrating on one—or at most two— aspects in each move. For example, you may need to accept a lower role to get into the right industry, or you may need to accept a position in the wrong company to elevate to a higher role. It's a bit of a juggle, and you will need to remain nimble to take advantage of opportunities when they occur, but here is one way it could work out. Let's assume, as suggested above, that you are an online retail sales manager with dreams of being CEO of a legacy airline. It would be unrealistic to map out a plan for specific positions in specific companies at specific dates with specific salaries, but you can still have SMART goals by planning your path as follows.

BASELINE: START WHERE YOU ARE

You're managing a team of sales representatives, developing sales strategies, and meeting revenue targets. So think of the skills you've developed in this role, and plan how they can take you one step closer to your goal. You feel confident that you can list leadership, negotiation, customer relationship management, and some strategic planning as skills gained. So plan your next move to take advantage of these.

Step 1: Promotion to Regional Sales Director

This is not a huge leap. You're in the same company, so you know the ropes, but you're being given more responsibilities. It's a chance to shine, to show that you take your career seriously. This is an opportunity to enhance your talents, adding multiregional management, strategic oversight, and advanced data analysis to your skillset.

Step 2: Promotion to Head of Sales

This is not an overambitious move. You've gained experience in the company, so now you are ready to learn cross-functional leadership and lead the entire sales department, collaborate with marketing and product teams, and drive overall sales strategy. It's a chance to prove that you have strategic vision and can make high-level decisions.

Step 3: Promotion to Vice President of Sales and Marketing

The C-suite is in your sights. This is a position with real authority. You will be managing both sales and marketing functions, integrating sales strategies with marketing campaigns, and driving revenue growth. It's a chance to learn the finer details of integrated strategy development and brand management. This will be your first executive-level role.

Step 4: Sideways Shift to Vice President of Sales and Marketing for a Hotel Group

This is not a promotion, and you may even need to take a salary cut, but it will be worth it in the end. It's not a move up, but it is a move sideways that gets you closer to your goal. Your duties are likely to be similar—managing sales and marketing functions, integrating sales strategies with marketing campaigns, and driving revenue growth—but the learning opportunities are priceless. It's a foot in the door in the tourism industry, so you will learn about seasonality and get the chance to plan joint marketing campaigns with destination marketing organizations and—yes—incoming airlines.

Step 5: Promotion to Chief Commercial Officer (CCO)

This one is a big deal. It's your first real C-suite role, and the stakes are getting higher. This is your opportunity to enhance your long-term strategic planning skills, develop comprehensive commercial oversight, and implement executive team collaboration.

You will be overseeing all commercial activities, including sales, marketing, and customer service. More importantly, you will be responsible for developing long-term commercial strategies with other tourism stakeholders, including airlines.

Step 6: Sideways Shift to Chief Operating Officer (COO) of a Regional Low-Cost Airline

Almost there. This may be a small airline but the skills you learn and the contacts you make will be invaluable. You'll be responsible for managing day-to-day operations, ensuring operational efficiency, and implementing strategic initiatives across the organization. Basically, you'll be keeping the planes in the air.

This may well be your biggest learning curve career move. As well as operational management, process optimization, and organizational leadership, you'll learn about working with flight schedules, time zones, and aeronautical law. You will forge connections with other airlines and airplane manufacturers. As COO, you will work closely with the marketing team and local destination management organizations. You will get the opportunity to meet other airline executives at international tourism and aeronautical trade shows.

Step 7: A Strategic Demotion to Vice President of Sales and Marketing for a National Legacy Airline

This may look like you're moving backwards, but you will really just be moving one step down in order to move across. It could be risky because you have exchanged the right role for the right company, but it could be a good move. Your responsibilities will not be onerous because you have the experience, and that means you can excel. You'll be managing sales and marketing functions, integrating sales strategies with marketing campaigns, and driving revenue growth. This might seem like a backward move but it isn't because you have your foot in the door of the desired company. It's an opportunity to use your understanding of tourism and connections with airplane manufacturers. Your new company will be flying to more and further destinations, so you will gain a greater understanding of international law. It's an opportunity to shine.

Step 8: Elevate to Chief Operating Officer (COO) of the Same National Legacy Airline

Yes, it was worth taking that downwards and sideways step. You're in the same role you were in two jobs ago, but you're in the right company. You'll be managing day-to-day operations, ensuring operational efficiency, and implementing strategic initiatives across the organization. You'll be using and refining all the skills you learned in the smaller airline but on a much bigger scale.

Step 9: Appointment as CEO of the Same National Legacy Airline

Stepping up from COO to CEO may seem like you've finally made it. And you have, but that doesn't mean you can be complacent. Your responsibilities will increase exponentially. You'll be responsible for overall leadership, strategic direction, and organizational success. You will represent the company to internal and external stakeholders, and generally, be the person with whom the buck stops.

AND FURTHER STEPS

I said earlier that the journey is the destination, which is true. But guess what? The destination is also the journey. Just because you've reached the C-suite doesn't mean you stop growing. Don't stop learning, because as Albert Einstein once said: "When you stop learning, you start dying."

IS IT REALLY SMART?

Yes, it is. While the above trajectory isn't absolutely prescriptive, it is **specific**. The plan is to work to your strengths and stay in sales, while gaining experience in companies associated with your ultimate goal. It's also **measurable** because you will either be in that position or not. It's **achievable** because you have not unrealistically dreamed about being CEO of Virgin Atlantic in two years. It's definitely **relevant** because you have specified industries or sectors that work closely with airlines. And it's clearly **time-bound**.

Setting and achieving SMART goals requires discipline—modified by modification. You can apply the concept of discipline and modification to any of your activities. Discipline is not taking time off or making excuses. You can apply discipline in your routine, whatever that routine looks like, and wherever you are. For example, if you have a routine of reading educational books for an hour every day, but you are traveling or if your schedule only allows for limited time to read, take whatever time is available. And if necessary, modify it. If you will be somewhere you can't access your digital library or there is no power, you may need to modify your tasks to take into account the limitations by, perhaps, taking a printed book with you. Align the plan with the realities of your situation.

A LEADERSHIP MINDSET

Developing a dynamic leadership mindset will enable you to respond to the current state and the future state. The leadership mindset is a belief that your abilities, your intelligence, and your potential can be cultivated to create understanding, learning, and perseverance, and to improve the situations, people, and processes around us. A leadership mindset can work in the moment—the current state—while mentally and physically moving towards the future—the future state. Some of the key factors that will help you create and maintain a leadership mindset are:

- **Continuous learning**: Pursuing advanced education (e.g., MBA), attending industry conferences, and staying updated on industry trends
- **Mentorship and networking**: Building relationships with senior leaders, seeking mentorship, and expanding professional networks
- **Proven track record**: Demonstrating consistent success in previous roles, achieving targets, and driving growth
- **Leadership development**: Participating in leadership development programs and taking on challenging projects to build leadership skills
- **Adaptability and innovation**: Being open to new ideas, embracing change, and driving innovation within the organization

BEYOND THE PERSONAL

While this is your path to your ultimate destination, and it's about your career, you need to look beyond your own personal needs. Once you have mapped out your personal plan, you need to align it with the business goals and objectives of your existing organization. You cannot plan to succeed in the future by neglecting to plan for success every day, in the here and now. It is only by succeeding in your current situation that you will get to move forward to your inevitable outcome.

It's time to make that plan a reality—to put the plan into words and put those words into action.

SPEAK YOUR POWER

Words are more than a way to communicate with other people. Words have power. Did you know that "abracadabra" is not just Hogwarts mumbo jumbo? It comes from an Aramaic phrase that means "it will be created as it is said." It is by verbalizing our thoughts and dreams that we bring them to fruition. That is why I advise my clients to write their goals, their life maps, and their strategies in their journals. That's why people create vision boards because images are a part of language. It's also why parents think so long and so hard before deciding on a name for a child. The concept of nominative determinism— that people's names determine their role in life—may not be a scientific truth, but it makes for great predinner conversation and there might be something to it. Although, if there is, it probably has more to do with the way people think about themselves than some mystical magical woo-woo.

Affirmations and goals need not be spoken out loud to be effective. Writing things down is also verbalizing—putting thoughts into words.

ACTIVATE THE PLAN

After speaking it, activate your plan by putting it into action. This means constantly striving for excellence day to day while planning for the future and actively following up with any opportunity. Use it or lose it. And while we're tossing around clichés, fake it till you make it. Clichés became clichés because they vividly and succinctly encapsulate universal truths, so don't knock them.

In the spirit of "fake it till you make it," dress for success, walk the walk, and talk the talk. Even if you're the procurement manager, dress like a CEO, act like a CEO, and talk like a CEO. That's what will help you become the store manager and then the regional manager and then, ultimately, the CEO. Faking it until you make it is a proactive strategy for starting to live the life you aspire to; it's not pretending to be something you're not. It's a fine distinction, but the best measure of whether you are faking it or actually being a fake is how comfortable you feel. If you can't imagine yourself wearing a tie or high heels, work around it. Step out of your comfort zone but only just. Swap your Birkenstocks for elegant flats or wear a smart, neatly pressed shirt and a sports coat rather than a suit and tie. If you hate skirts and dresses, wear a smart pants suit. And talking like a CEO does not mean ordering people around. It means speaking with confidence, and speaking with confidence is most easily achieved by thinking before you open your mouth. It's a mindset.

I put this into practice when I first started working. I was doing door-to-door sales, but I deliberately emulated the owner of the company. I wore a suit and tie and I carried a smart briefcase. I dressed for success: I wore CEO shoes and I carried a CEO briefcase. It was one small part of the plan that got me to where I wanted to be.

EXECUTE THE PLAN

You are reading this book because you are determined to find your spot in the C-suite, and you know you are destined for executive management. But while you do have a specific end goal in mind, the destination is not really the C-suite, it's the journey. The journey is the destination. So yes, keep your mind on the goal, but keep your eye on the ball. Every step, every move, no matter how small, is more than just preparation for the end goal. It's an integral part of the destination. So practice, practice, practice.

Accelerate the plan consistent with your stated goals and objectives. Consider what you are doing and why you are doing it. Every day. Be consistent, be tenacious, and move one step closer to your goal, one step further along your journey, every single day. And when you reach the C-suite, you will realize you are still on the journey. Don't stop now. Practice, practice, practice, and keep developing and nurturing your superpower.

NURTURE YOUR SUPERPOWER

Living in your superpower is about living consciously every day, being present, communicating effectively, and nurturing connections with your colleagues, your community, your family, and your friends. It's about creating interdependent relationships with mentors and protégées, but it's also about ensuring you get enough me-time—time to recharge.

Communicate how you execute and implement plans, goals, and objectives. Most importantly, reward yourself and reward others. It's all about maintaining your personal effectiveness and performance and ensuring that every team you work with is equally effective.

In the spirit of knowing that the journey is the destination, never stop planning, never stop improving, always have new goals and new objectives, and always come up with new strategies for achieving them.

BE TRUE TO YOURSELF: GH GROWS WITH THE JOB

My client GH worked his way up from the bottom by sheer grit, determination, and discipline. He grew up on a farm in a blue-collar community in the Midwest and was the first person in his family to go to university. He had to work his way through college tending bar, and when he graduated, he got a job in sales, which delighted both him and his family. At the time, he considered this an indication of having made it.

He worked hard, always showed up, always delivered. Having no influential friends or family who could mentor him, he learned on the job, and to his surprise, he was soon promoted to sales manager. He knew he was good at his job, but he was a modest person from a humble background, and he didn't feel comfortable in a management role. However, after a while in management, he realized that his inevitable destiny was the C-suite and not the sales floor, so he decided he needed coaching. He had discovered a burning desire to succeed, not only for himself, but also to lead by example and help others replicate his success for themselves.

Together, we assessed where he was and how he'd gotten there, and then mapped out a plan for him to get where he wanted to be. Already, he was in a whole new headspace, having elevated himself from a role in which he was successful but not really challenged to a new role with many challenges.

After a detailed SWOT analysis, he visualized himself doing something that he'd had no experience with or exposure to. It was all new to him, so I told him, "Fake it till you make it." I advised him to dress, talk, and act like a CEO, but he couldn't see himself in a CEO-level designer suit and tie with super shiny Italian shoes. So he found a great middle ground. He swapped his chamois shirts, jeans, and sneakers for neat button-down Oxford shirts, comfortable but tailored slacks, and leather loafers that were elegant but still practical. He looked middle management, rather than sales floor. He was making a statement: "I am elevating to another level." But he was still himself.

He realized that he needed help from within the organization. He needed a mentor, but he had always felt intimidated in the presence of senior management. So I advised him to actively seek out people who could advise him, rather than trying to figure things out on his own. It took a while, but he overcame his reticence and started to communicate with people at the highest level in his organization. By showing willingness to learn and advance, he won the ear of the president of the company, who has been mentoring him now for two years.

After working as sales manager for three years, he was promoted to division manager in the same company and then—after another two years, to national sales manager for the whole United States. He is not in the C-suite yet, but it is in sight. He is well and truly set on the path to his inevitable outcome. And, along with his career elevation, his taste in clothes has evolved to match his status. He looks good in a well-cut suit, and more importantly, he feels good wearing one.

Leaders are most impactful through meticulous preparation, expert delivery, stage presence, engaging communication, and credibility.

Chapter 6

EXPECT THE UNEXPECTED

A bend in the road is not the end of the road...unless you
fail to make the turn.
–Helen Keller

All trail runners know that having a fixed idea of where your feet are going to land is the surest way to stumble. The secret to running safely over rough terrain is to look a few yards ahead and keep your knees and ankles loose and ready to land when and where they will. It makes no difference whether your foot lands on a root, a loose pebble, or solid ground because you're already lifting it as it lands. Well, the business world is also rough terrain where threats and obstacles will arise, so to keep from stumbling you need to be flexible and open to change—look ahead and be ready to change direction mid stride.

BEING SIDELINED HURTS

Jalen Hurts was benched on the biggest stage in college football. One minute he was the face of Alabama. The next, he was standing on the sidelines watching someone else finish what he started.

In 2016, he began his collegiate career at the University of Alabama, where he quickly made a name for himself as a talented and versatile quarterback who could perform well under pressure. He led Alabama's Crimson Tide to victory in the 2016 Southeastern Conference (SEC) Championship. The team's perfect 12–0 season put them in the running for the 2017 Sugar Bowl championship. Hurts's face was seen nationally, smiling from the cover of the College Football Playoff special edition of *Sports Illustrated.* He was riding high.

But then everything changed.

In the 2017 National Championship game, Hurts was benched at halftime in favor of Tua Tagovailoa, who led the team to victory. To Hurts, it must have felt like he'd had the championship snatched away from him at the last minute after putting in all that work in 2016. This is a not uncommon occurrence in the corporate world, and how you handle it defines your professional trajectory. Hurts used the setback as motivation to improve. He remained a loyal teammate and practiced hard, but unfortunately, he stayed on the bench the whole season. Despite putting a brave face on it, he realized that this was a disaster. How were the NFL scouts going to find him if he wasn't on the field? So, while not burning any bridges, he made the changes necessary for his career, and in his senior year, transferred to the University of Oklahoma, where he thrived.

In retrospect, his season on the bench demonstrated his class and resilience showing that he could handle setbacks with grace and that he was open to change. And it was noticed. In the second round of the 2020 NFL Draft, he was drafted by the Philadelphia Eagles as a backup to their superstar quarterback, Carson Wentz. Even though it was expected that Wentz would remain the Eagles' quarterback for at least a few years, he was injured in 2020, and Hurts took over as quarterback. Although he faced numerous challenges, including injuries, Hurts led the iconic Eagles franchise with style and confidence. His setback at Alabama had taught him to prepare for the unexpected, so he approached every game with careful planning, and his training and preparation were characterized by strict discipline and hard work. His work ethic and focus on constantly improving his mental and physical skills formed a solid base from which he developed the leadership qualities that were to take the Eagles to Super Bowl stardom.

The rest is history. Philadelphia beat the Kansas City Chiefs 40–22 in the 2025 Super Bowl, and Hurts was named most valuable player. Yes, it's not the C-suite, and football might be called a game by some, but I think the story of Jalen Hurts is fitting here because—let's be honest—quarterbacks are the CEOs of sports, and his journey to the virtual C-suite of football is a testament to his ability to overcome challenges and rise above deep disappointment to become a Super Bowl-winning MVP. Also, football is a business, so leading a team of the Eagles' standing is good preparation for a career off the field.

Hurts is using his skills, determination, and discipline to craft an investment and career trajectory that will take him beyond the expected brand endorsements and collaborations. With a growing personal brand and investments in technology, wellness, real estate, and more, he is well on the way to his inevitable outcome as a successful business leader. After all, professional football is a young man's game, so he can't play at that level forever.

STAY READY SO YOU CAN BE READY

I have a client who is very skilled at her core competencies, but she lacks confidence in public speaking—particularly in front of large groups. So we are intentional about putting her in situations where she speaks to big and small groups—even if it's the opening statement or introducing the main speaker. That way, if she is asked to address a board meeting or press conference at the last minute, she'll be ready because she's had that experience already. She is staying ready so that she'll be ready, and she's learning that by consciously stepping out of her comfort zone.

Expecting the unexpected also means embracing your experiences—all of them, good and bad—and taking losses as lessons to be learned. It's about regularly practicing the hard things and operating in hard places. Practicing hard things means doing what you're uncomfortable with and stepping out of your comfort zone. That way you'll be ready when circumstances change, and your working environment becomes more challenging. *Stay* ready so you don't have to *get* ready. And when things fall apart and everyone else is running around like a headless chicken, you can stand up calmly and deliver the ultimate clichéd response: "I was born ready."

SEEING 'ROUND CORNERS

You can see there's a bend in the road before you get there, so you can prepare for it, but you can't see what's around the corner. That's because the unexpected *is* unexpected, so you can't plan for it, you can only prepare for it and be ready to think on your feet.

As a top executive, you will need to strategize nationally and internationally, and that requires a global perspective and attempting to foresee what's coming. Of course, no one can predict global markets, foreign policy, and international conflicts in advance, but you do need to pay attention to what is happening in the world and at least play with some possible scenarios to ensure you and your organization are resilient and flexible.

It's an accurate cliché that hindsight is 20/20, but that doesn't help us predict the future. Or does it? Of course, the future will not be exactly like the past, but we can learn from history. Imagine for a moment you were alive and the head of a large corporation on June 30, 1914. You may have read in the paper about the assassination of Archduke Franz Ferdinand of Austria two days previously, but you certainly would not have reacted in horror and exclaimed, "Oh no, this is the beginning of World War One." Of course not, that would be ridiculous.

However, if you'd had a globalist perspective, you may have noticed Russia's eastern expansion and war with Japan from 1904 to 1905, Austria-Hungary's annexation of Bosnia and Herzegovina in 1908, Italy's invasion of Libya in 1911, and a squabble between France and Germany over Morocco in the same year. And if you'd been very perceptive, you'd have noted that Germany had been expanding its navy at an unprecedented rate for decades.

If you'd been in a serious leadership position then, you should have been considering the possibility that Europe was not that stable. And if you'd had any doubts, the Balkan Wars of 1912 and 1913 should have clinched it. So the assassination of Archduke Ferdinand did not really cause the war; it was merely the match that lit the well-laid tinder. Like Covid and the 2008 financial crisis, these supposedly black swans rapidly faded to white once they'd been analyzed with a bit of thought and hindsight. They were obvious in retrospect. So while you can't see 'round corners, you can see the bends ahead and navigate them in a way that prepares you for what's just out of sight, even perhaps giving you an inkling of what to expect.

What do you think people will be saying about today's political and socioeconomic conditions in ten or twenty years? You can't predict for sure but consider the possibilities. And while you're doing that, don't forget to plan for tomorrow, next week, next quarter, and next year. You'll need effective processes to deal with whatever life, the weather, the international community, and your own personal circumstances throw at you.

Resilience is not about withstanding change and fighting off challenges, it's about being sufficiently flexible to ride them and to keep dancing when the beat changes. Resilience is like learning to surf so that you don't get tumbled by the waves and drown. Rather, you ride them to a safe shore and possibly a better future. That requires preparation and skill.

Like I always tell my clients, many things are out of our control, but process pulverizes problems, so prepare for problems by prioritizing process. Of course, managing business processes is an important part of resilience, but so is health and emotional stability. Take time every day to stay ahead of the game. Exercise, eat well, hydrate sufficiently, and hone your process. Most important, stay informed so that you can adapt as circumstances change. Don't be a one-trick pony because they don't last long in the circus ring, so their choices are limited— and so is their future.

In the same way that doomsday preppers keep a go bag packed with food and medical supplies, keep a virtual go bag at the ready—a combination of your physical health, your financial stability, your emotional and intellectual preparedness, and your process. Stay ready so you don't have to get ready.

MANAGE MISHAPS

So when the wheels do fall off, when the sky does fall, and life as we know it is over, what do we do? We could run and panic like Chicken Little but that would probably get us eaten by a fox. As I said above, we need to be resilient, and we can access resilience only from within. We need to use our innate gifts, our superpowers, to focus and implement processes. We all have the materials to create, develop, and build resilience. You have to be self-aware to know that you have the raw materials to recreate the new you. That takes us right back to discovering and developing our inner resources, as outlined in chapters 2 and 3. You have the internal materials, so all you have to do is realize and access your inherent toughness. This is when your superpower comes to the fore. You may surprise yourself because many people don't realize how powerful their superpowers are until they are faced with real challenges. It's a bit like the urban myth of a mother single-handedly lifting a bus to save her child.

The external factors threatening you, your position, and your organization may be one of the dragons we identified in chapter 4, but they may also belong to an entirely new species of dragon that has never before been encountered. If that's the case, just fall back on the process, because—it's worth repeating—the process pulverizes problems. Perhaps you need to keep a pretty pink, problem-pulverizing dragon of perfect process as a pet.

It's important to have a process for dealing with potential problems, but sometimes things still go horribly wrong, and when they do, we need to change tactics. Johnny Cash, who knew a few things about failure, advised that you build on it and use it as a stepping stone. Winston Churchill, who knew a few things about success, described it as "stumbling from failure to failure with no loss of enthusiasm." Even when things don't go according to plan, you can still pick up the pieces and carry on.

RECOVER FROM SETBACKS

It's all very well saying you have the internal fortitude to overcome any obstacle, and that your superpower will enable you to lift mythical buses off imaginary children, but sometimes things really do go wrong. Sometimes we lose our jobs, the company we work for goes bankrupt, the town we're living in is washed away in a flood, or our supply chain is severely disrupted by war, weather, or Wall Street. These things do happen, and when they do, you just have to get back into the metaphorical saddle. If you're wondering how to do that, go back to the beginning of this chapter. It's all there. Resilience is not a destination, it's a journey. It's a process and—yes, I'll say it again—using process pulverizes problems.

NEVER WASTE A GOOD CRISIS

I suppose we shouldn't consider hurricanes to be unexpected because we have, on average, seven per year in the United States. We have a pretty good idea they will happen, we just don't know when or where. At least not exactly. So when Hurricane Helene trashed much of North Carolina in September 2024, it wasn't a surprise. What was surprising, though, was the extent of the damage valued at almost $80 billion. One of the companies that was hardest hit was the IV manufacturer, Baxter—and the ramifications were immense. Baxter was the country's biggest manufacturer of intravenous equipment and supplies, so when Helene's accompanying floods roared through the factory, the repercussions were felt in healthcare facilities nationwide. Which brings me to my client B. Braun Medical Inc.

Braun was the second-largest manufacturer of IV equipment and solutions in the USA, and until September 2024, one of their main concerns was increasing market share. That's not surprising, since most companies aim at growth, and increasing market share is the surest way to achieve that.

But when Baxter stopped production, Braun's market more than tripled overnight. Now that may sound like a good thing, but it means that production had to increase threefold. Overnight. That's a big ask.

I had been coaching three of their executives—their head of sales, the global VP, and the CEO. This was an opportunity for them to step up and show how they could deal with the truly unexpected. Let's face it, many companies plan for a disaster knocking out their own manufacturing capacity, but how many plan for the same thing happening to their competitors?

The first thing I did was to ask all three of my clients what they thought, and each had a different perspective and a different way of approaching the problem. They were totally taken by surprise, but they'd had the experience of dealing with Covid when they also had to increase their output unexpectedly. While they'd had to speed up production during Covid, they were only one company among many, but Helene put them in a totally different position. All of a sudden, they were the biggest supplier of a vital product, so they had to expand their production even more rapidly, and it wasn't just internal. They had to look at the whole supply chain—their suppliers, their workforce, and their distribution. They had to procure raw materials from new companies, and start supplying hospitals they'd not done business with before.

We discussed the changes they made during Covid and I asked what they'd done then, when they knew they had to shift.

I pointed out that they were operating in extraordinary times so they had to consider the extra things needed to create extraordinary outcomes. First, we looked at the Covid protocol to see what we could use from the changes implemented during that time, and then adapted them for the existing challenge. We did a readiness mapping of what the plant could and should look like, balancing existing readiness with the proposed state. They had to bring in extra staff, increase outsourced support, find new suppliers, and negotiate extended logistics and distribution.

Each of my three clients took ownership of one of those pieces to come up with their portion of a single plan. So while each person was focusing on their own task, they also had to consider how those pieces connected with the ultimate readiness plan. They had to coordinate and collaborate to make sure that all the pieces were integrated.

This almost turned the old adage "every problem is an opportunity" on its head, in that in this case, the opportunity to increase market share was initially a problem, but only because they had not been prepared. Still, they were agile and flexible, so they managed to pivot and increase their output by 20% at their Irvine, California, and Daytona Beach, Florida, production facilities, and increase production at their Allentown, Pennsylvania, plant to produce more than 30 million additional IV sets in a year.

This was a bit short of the target of tripling production, but it was enough to keep hospitals operating throughout the country, thereby avoiding what could have been an absolute disaster. There was no way my clients could have predicted that their competition would cease production, but they managed to successfully overcome the unexpected challenges because they were flexible.

You can't control what happens to you, but you can control how you react to what happens to you.

PART 3

DISPLAY

Radiate so brightly that even your shadows shimmer.

You know you're on the fast track to the C-suite but you're not the only person on that track, and the sad truth is that not everyone who aims at the C-suite will eventually occupy it. So how can you ensure you're one of those who do? And, once there, how can you ensure that your incumbency will be memorable? It's time to display the superpower you've so cleverly discovered and so carefully developed. It's time to shine.

Chapter 7

STAND OUT FROM THE HERD

---

*Leaders should be seen **and** heard.*

You've done plenty of inward and outward personal exploration, discovered your superpower, and developed it into a useful tool. Now it's time to display it for the world to see. And by the world, of course, I mean potential employers and executive recruiters. I was a senior partner at Korn Ferry for six years, so I still have contacts in the executive recruitment field, and I have a pretty good idea of what recruiters are looking for.

CEDRIC CLARK SHINES—NOT JUST IN BUSINESS

Probably the last thing you expect of the executive vice president of a huge multinational like Walmart is that he'll sit down to play the piano for the board or the employees. Well, maybe the second to last, because the last thing you'd expect is that he would do it really well. Not just well, really well. But Cedric is full of surprises.

His management style is a testament to his dedication, curiosity, and leadership skills and his focus on continuous learning, teamwork, and investing in people. This approach has positioned him as a key leader in one of the world's largest retail organizations. You could say he's arrived, but he knows that the destination is another step in the journey, so he continues to engage his superpowers to show up, to knuckle down, to innovate, and to shine. And he does that by helping other people to shine. He constantly engages with people at the store level, investing in improving customer service by improving the employees' experience. He's redesigned the bonus programs and is constantly on the lookout for other ways to improve the overall Walmart experience for employees, customers, management, shareholders, board members, and all other stakeholders. He approaches everything with curiosity and determination so that he can, in his own words, "build reciprocal energy, grace, and connection to unlock our best selves, and others' best selves."

While ensuring that Walmart strategically maximizes any opportunities in the broader sense, he is intensely focused on helping all Walmart team members, and even people outside of the organization, to "rise and shine." One of his most effective innovations is Motivational Monday, a weekly practical video that provides insightful tips and leadership advice to help anyone maximize their own internal talent. While they are aimed primarily at Walmart team members, they can be found on LinkedIn, Facebook, and Instagram—reaching 50,000 followers. He continues to create inspirational and insightful podcasts, talk at important industry events, and appear as a guest on radio and TV interviews. More interestingly, he is in the process of documenting his Walmart Journey in a book he's coauthoring with me, so you will soon be able to read in more detail how he got to where he is and how he's maximized his impact in the role so far—how he shines.

And on that note, you're probably wondering about the piano playing. Yes, as well as being an exceptionally talented executive, Cedric is a professional-level concert pianist. He studied music at The Juilliard School, and while he never performed professionally, he has kept up the skill for his own pleasure and that of his friends and colleagues. So yes, sometimes he adds a planned—or even impromptu—performance to a board meeting or company event. It adds a very special something to his shine.

BEAT THE BOTS

AI is everywhere, including within recruitment. This is less of an issue for top-level executives, but if you are not there yet, you will need to successfully navigate BotLand to reach your inevitable outcome.

Top-Level Executive Jobs are Rarely Advertised

The job market is tough at every level but the challenges are different in that top-level executive jobs are rarely advertised. But the mid- or senior-level jobs that will form part of your career path may be, and they are likely to attract thousands of applicants. And here's where it gets scary. The first round of elimination is almost certainly done by a bot, so getting past that requires knowing how bots "think." But even that is not so simple. There are strategies for getting past the bot gatekeepers, and knowing those can put you ahead of the game. Sadly, though, AI changes strategy faster than marathon runners change socks. Can you see where this AI-fueled nightmare is heading? Obviously, you can't. No one can. But it's safe to assume that the bot's primary task will always be to figure out the quickest way to reduce a mountain of applications to something a human HR exec can manage. It will probably go through the CVs until it has selected its quota of perfect—or near-perfect—applications and then stop. So that brings us to the first rule of applying for advertised positions. Check for openings every single day and apply as soon as you see them.

Catch-22

The second rule of applying for advertised positions is forget the one-click easy-apply route. That's a great way to get very discouraged and deeply despondent because you can apply for 2,000 jobs, tailor your CV to each opportunity, reach out to the hiring managers, follow up with the recruiters, and still get nothing back.

The reality is that senior jobs rarely get advertised, and if they do, it's too late. Now you're competing on a level playing field with the 2,000 or 3,000 applicants for just a few spots, and it's first come, first served. Maybe you'll get lucky, but probably not.

Here's the catch-22: As you become more experienced and your experience becomes more diverse, you will never be a perfect match for anything. That's the bad news, but the good news is that every problem is an opportunity. Exceptionally talented people leave the herd where it's safe. They take risks by stepping out of their comfort zone and trying something new.

Inhabit the Real World

Yes, it's important to have an impressive online presence, but you also need to be visible in the real world. Go to PTA meetings at your kids' school, be active in your faith community, volunteer for public benefit organizations, and play golf— or choose a more contemporary option like yoga, Pilates, mountain biking, surfskiing, trail running or triathlons. This is important because many top-level jobs do not get advertised. Long before somebody in HR gets the instruction to write up a job profile, describe the metrics for selection, and then place the ad, someone around the boardroom table says, "This is our problem. Does anyone know somebody who could fix it for us?" And someone replies, "Oh, you know what, we should check in with so and so at Bank X. Because when I met her at the gym last week, she suggested she was feeling a bit frustrated with her current job." Probably 70% of senior hires get made like that. It's a disheartening truth, but that is how the world works, so—rule number one—network! (Yes, there are many rule number ones.)

Keep moving

To misquote the great Albert Einstein, life is like a bicycle— keep moving or you'll fall off. So don't stay in the same role in the same company too long. If you're not moving up—or at least strategically sideways—every couple of years, recruiters will assume you have no ambition.

Don't Stagnate

Even if you are being constantly promoted, be wary about staying in the same company too long—unless, of course, it's the company you ultimately want to head up. And even if it is, a stint in another company may be a good strategic move. Of course, it's not a hard science, so you'll need to think on your feet. What seems like a good idea in some situations may be terrible in others. There are exceptions, but generally, people who don't move around don't move up.

Recruiters are wary of people who've been in the same company for years, even if they have been constantly promoted. There's always the suspicion that they've become institutionalized. You need to show that you can easily move into new situations, gel with new teams, and take on new challenges. Of course, you need to balance this with loyalty, so be careful when switching companies. Make sure you leave things neat and tidy for the next incumbent. Leaving a company halfway through an important project is not wise.

There is a caveat and this may sound contradictory, but you can get away with staying in the same company if it has many divisions and you've consistently been promoted and moved from one division to another. If you've moved between different cities, states, countries, or continents, so much the better. It's about working with different teams, different suppliers, and different clients. It's about showing that you're not sitting in a comfort zone, happily feeding marshmallows to the cute, cuddly dragon of complacency.

Most importantly, though, you have to be proactive about finding your next role.

PUT YOURSELF OUT THERE

Move in the right circles in the real world. Playing golf and being involved in your community is good, but you need to do more. Attend professional events, speak at conferences, comment on matters in your field, and generally, be the go-to person for an authoritative perspective. More importantly, if you want something, go after it. With focus. Proactively approach companies and executive recruiters, cultivate media contacts, and spend time doing volunteer work, either as a board member of public benefit organizations or as a hands-on volunteer at high-profile events.

Proactively Approach Potential Companies

One of my recruitment contacts told me how she carved her own career.

> I know how recruitment works. So my last two jobs, I skipped all of it. I got hold of the CEO and sold myself on one phone call with the stuff that I knew they would want to hear. I told them how much revenue I was generating as a result of my business development work, and why I wanted to work for them. They would have been idiots not to interview me. I've only done it twice, and it worked both times.

So, craft a marketing call you can use with prospective employers. It could go something like this:

> Hi. My name's Bobby Smith. We haven't met, but I'm a senior procurement manager currently working at X Company. I've got ten years experience in retail buying and logistics. I'm great at streamlining supply chains, as evidenced by the fact that my company's turnover increased by X last year, while the logistics expenses decreased by Y. I'm looking for my next role. I've done my research, and your company looks like the kind of place I would really thrive. Can we set a time to chat?

Once having set up that meeting, though, be sure to follow through. A recruiter I know told me a story about a man who'd been looking for a job for three years. We'll call him PCV, and we'll catch up with him later. He's read books on how to find a job, he's polished his LinkedIn profile to a high gloss, and his CV is spectacularly impressive and can be easily optimized for specific roles. He's researched 200 companies that are perfect for him, he's following 50 job boards, and is applying for up to three jobs a day. He's putting in a lot of time and energy proactively contacting people. He's having coffee meetings with all the right people, and he's telling them what his capabilities are.

So, the recruiter asked him, "While you're telling these executives what you can do and what experience you have, have you actually asked for a job? Have you said you'd like to work for them?"

"No," he replied. "That seems a bit forward."

And that's why all he gets out of these coffee meetings is a cappuccino and perhaps the advice, "You should try Company X, I hear they're looking."

The moral of this story is obvious. Ask for what you want. Executive-level managers need to be proactive and take risks. PCV had taken the first step in approaching people, but he was treating the meetings as social events because he was afraid to close the deal and ask for what he wanted. Be brave and don't let the masked imposter syndrome dragon follow you to your meetings. Lock it in the garage before you leave home.

Another way of approaching a potential company is to offer to solve a problem, but this can be risky because it requires that you tell them they are not perfect. But it may be worth a shot. Your initial pitch could go something like this:

> Hi. My name's Alex Alexis. We haven't met, but I've been trying to return an item I bought from your company. I was not happy with the response, so I took a closer look at your CRM process and noticed that your follow-up on complaints generates more complaints, and some queries go unresolved for as long as two weeks. I can improve this by doing X, Y, and Z to optimize complaint resolution and A, B, and C to automate response delegation to the relevant CRM agents. I have already done something similar for Top to Bottom Design Studio, and for my previous client, Side-to-Side Solutions. I'm a customer relations consultant dealing mostly with

> online retail companies, and I believe I can improve your customer retention ratio and save you up to X hundred thousand dollars a year from lost revenue due to customer dissatisfaction.

It's a risky one. On the one hand, you're telling them they're making a mistake, which they probably already know. But in the process of doing that, you're not making them feel great. So even though they may agree that it needs to be fixed, they might not want you to be the one to fix it. I know someone who tried this strategy, and the response was a polite thank you. And then two months later, a competitor was invited to pitch a solution, using the very same criteria, proving this point. They wanted the problem solved, but not by the person who had pointed it out. So yes, it's an option, but one to be approached very cautiously.

If you don't feel comfortable approaching companies directly, you could approach executive recruiters, but that's not as simple as it sounds. Other strategies for being seen include cultivating media contacts and volunteering for the boards of public benefits to ensure that your name is publicly linked with your field of expertise.

Approach Executive Recruiters—Carefully

Most executive search companies work on a brief from organizations and then go out and actively look for suitable candidates. So most of them don't welcome approaches from potential candidates. Even if they do, remember they will not act as agents on your behalf. The most you can expect is that they will put your CV on file and think of you if and when they need someone with your skills and experience.

Some recruitment companies nurture these unsolicited candidates, so they have a pool of highly qualified people they can refer to before they go to the trouble of looking further. It's also particularly handy to have a pool of highly qualified, currently unemployed people for unexpected requests. For example, a client may call in a flurry because their CFO has just had a serious bicycle accident and will be in the hospital in traction for two months.

If the agency can fill that void in a few days, everybody wins.

Cultivate Media Contacts

Actively seek out journalists, writers, radio producers, influencers, and other media professionals in your field and in your community. Be the person they call for comment if there's a flood, a stock market wobble, a new type of widget, or a building collapse. Don't underestimate the value of potential employers reading, viewing, or hearing, "Oh, you know, this has just happened so we're going to speak to Joe Soap, the XYZ manager of X Company for their opinion about how this will impact the market share of ABC."

Journalists are busy people so they appreciate having someone "in their back pocket" they can call for a quote, comment, or explanation. So, carefully cultivate them. Write op-eds for print media and on relevant websites, and comment on relevant platforms. If your comments are particularly insightful, they'll start calling you.

Volunteer

A beautiful way to elevate your leadership profile is to do volunteer work for nonprofits and public benefit organizations with an eye to getting a seat on the board. For maximum impact, choose an organization related to your field. It's an opportunity to use your expertise to benefit an organization, but it also benefits you because it brings more visibility and indicates empathy, compassion, and leadership. It shows that you are a well-rounded person with diverse interests and concerns. And of course, volunteering on a board gives you executive-level management experience, even if it's not in a big commercial company.

The above strategies are essential, but if you are to be noticed, you need to inhabit the virtual world as well as the actual physical one.

BE SOCIAL, BE SEEN

Gone are the days when executive recruiters picked up the phone and snooped around to get information about prospective appointees. It's not ethical or very effective because it's so much easier to access their public profiles. Anybody at an executive leadership level should have a visible personal brand, and the first place recruiters look is LinkedIn.

The best thing you can do is have a strong, visible public profile. That's really where the magic is. We live in the age of social media and if you are not visible, you're dead in the water.

Sanitize Your Social Media

Before you even think of enhancing your professional online image, take a long, hard look at your personal online presence. It's astonishing how many really intelligent people have trashed their careers through one silly, thoughtless tweet, post, or even a passively tagged photo. Sanitize your social media like it is carrying the love child of Covid and Ebola. Here are some pointers, some of which are so obvious, they should go without saying but you would be surprised...

- Don't troll. Seriously. Just don't. Comment if you must, but be polite. Feel free to disagree, but disagree respectfully.
- Don't "other." This should go without saying, but if you have opinions that can even slightly be interpreted as racist, sexist, homophobic, xenophobic (or any other isms or phobics), keep them to yourself. Be squeaky clean.
- Think before you like or forward anything. Read something through carefully before you glibly endorse it. A post that starts as a sensible comment on consumer issues may morph into a racist rant halfway through.
- Scrutinize any photos you post. Read the poster in the background of that pic of you and your bestie having coffee, and if necessary, photoshop it out. Hey, if in doubt, photoshop it out.
- Ensure you are appropriately dressed in all photos. You don't need to limit your online photos to professional suit-and-tie portraits but ensure you are neatly dressed, and sufficiently covered. Is a beach pic really what you want the world to see?

- Be careful who can tag you. We are all human and we need to let our hair down, but you don't want a pic of you knocking back martinis at your best friend's bachelorette party to surface online. While it's nothing to be ashamed of, it's not the image you want out there for prospective employers to see.
- Obviously, you are entitled to opinions about religion and politics, but keep comments about them respectful and nonconfrontational. The same goes for sports. It's OK to celebrate the team you support but treat all rival teams and supporters with respect.
- Steer away from conspiracy theories. Feel free to believe the British royal family are lizards, the moon landings were faked, the Covid vaccine was designed by Bill Gates to take over our minds, and Elvis and Jim Morrison are alive and well living on some island paradise, but keep it to yourself.
- Don't diss your boss or your company online. This is obvious, but you would be surprised how many people do and then wonder why they are unemployed.

Perfect Your LinkedIn Profile

LinkedIn is your shop window and yours has to be perfect. It's the first place recruiters look. I cannot emphasize how important this is. But here's an important caveat. The world changes quickly, and the online, social media world changes even more quickly. So some time soon, LinkedIn may become yesterday's tech. Or not. But be prepared. Yes, right now it's the most powerful platform for career enhancement, but keep an eye out for new developments and take advantage of new channels sooner rather than later. It doesn't mean you have to abandon the old, tried and tested ones—at least not while they're still working. Stay agile.

Curate Connections

Your connections are an important part of your LinkedIn profile, but be careful of going for quantity over quality. We've all had invitations from absolute strangers before, and when you look at their profile, you see they have 17,834 connections. Really? Nope. These are just people who blindly accepted their random invites, so they are not real connections. Real connections—literally—indicate how connected you are, while arbitrary fake connections indicate how desperate you are to appear connected. There is a big difference.

So don't accept invitations from strangers. Rethink who is a stranger and who is not. If you get an invite from someone you don't know, check their shared connections. If they are first-degree connections of seven or eight people you know well and often do business with, that's a great sign—they're likely a good connection for you.

And regularly go through the list of suggested connections that LinkedIn generates. Some may be people you know really well and are not connected with, but some—much like above—may be people on the periphery of your circle and may be very useful contacts. Only connect with someone you can check up on, even through a shared connection, so that you can be sure they are who they say they are and that they have achieved what they say they have.

Check out those third-degree connections, especially if they are influential or strategically important. Is there a way you can enhance your connectivity before you invite them to connect? For example, you may have no actual connections in common but you can say in the invite, "We met at the Environmentally Responsible Mining Summit in Cape Town, where I was particularly interested in your presentation about progressive rehabilitation and mine closure planning."

LinkedIn is about extending your network, so take advantage of every constructive opportunity and always prioritize quality over quantity.

Keep Active on Social Media

OK, so you have the perfect social media presence. Your educational and employment history is up to date, and your profile pic is professional and flattering. Why are the job offers not rolling in? Possibly because you're not coming up on searches. If you are not optimizing your profile, you're likely to get lost in the clutter. Take, for example, LinkedIn.

You probably know that LinkedIn works with algorithms, so when a recruiter searches for a specific type of person with specific experience, the algorithms do their magic and come up with some suggestions. But what you may not know is if you have not been active on your profile, it "disappears." It doesn't get deleted, and people can still search for you by name but it becomes less visible. Every time someone posts on their profile, the algorithms take note, and that profile rises in the rankings. What this means is that if there are two equally qualified profiles, the most active one will be at the top of the list. So the longer you remain inactive, the deeper your profile will sink into the murk, until in effect, it's invisible. The technical term is dormant. And dormant basically means dead. That's why you have to keep active on LinkedIn.

Don't Promote Yourself, Engage

Being active on LinkedIn and other social media sites can be a double-edged sword. As Mark Twain so succinctly said, "It is better to keep your mouth closed and let people think you are a fool than to open it and remove all doubt." But with LinkedIn, that's not the case. You do need to be active, to comment, and to engage. But—bearing in mind Twain's wise advice—do so carefully. Don't try to promote yourself. Instead, be visible by supporting others. (This strategy can work offline as well.)

Comment positively on other people's posts, follow people who have something positive to say, and congratulate connections on achievements. Endorse your connections for skills in which they excel and don't be shy about asking for endorsements in return—but obviously only from people who know you and what you can do.

Post Useful Professional Advice and Information

One of the most effective ways of enhancing your LinkedIn profile is to post useful articles such as succinct advice on how to build your brand, increase customer engagement, or prevent fires. It's also useful to post milestones, e.g., "We laid the foundation for the second phase of the Chicago Convention Center last week." And add photos, preferably with you in them.

While the above strategies are designed to make you stand out, it's important to not stand out too much.

STAND OUT BUT BLEND IN

We are hardwired to trust people who are similar to us, which is why racism has had such a good run. Fortunately, though, we have evolved as a society to realize that people can *be* like us even if they don't *look* like us. It's about values and experience. Let's face it, even the most egalitarian of HR managers would not consider someone without an engineering degree for an engineering job, and you really do want the person who takes out your appendix to be a qualified surgeon. So if the most trusted profiles are the ones that are most like the recruiters or existing senior executives, does that mean that people with a different ethnicity or who went to different schools stand no chance? Fortunately it doesn't, but if you want to "join the club," you need to show that you respect the club's rules.

Highlight Your Superpower

Remember PCV? The guy who took dozens of executives out for coffee but was too shy to ask for what he wanted? He has experience in a wide range of industries, but he has been doing low paying consultancy work way below his level of expertise. He's put together a spreadsheet with a list of things that will help him stand out from the crowd to get a job. He's highly qualified—but that's part of the problem. He genuinely could step into almost any senior role in any industry, but nobody puts out a job description for someone who can do everything.

He hasn't identified his superpower, or if he has, he's not focusing on it.

So be deliberate about emphasizing your superpower, while keeping your other not-so-superpower skills in reserve. You could say, "My superpower is numbers. I can reduce anything to a conversation about return on investment and do the math in a moment."

If you have other skills that may be valuable, you can mention them later, but don't let them take the focus away from your superpower, because it is your superpower that will eclipse differences—not disguise differences, not lie about them, eclipse them. If your superpower is sufficiently well-developed and properly displayed, your race, age, ethnicity, religion, or sexual orientation will not only be irrelevant, it will go unnoticed. It will "disappear" like the sun disappears behind the moon during an eclipse.

Follow the Rules

Regardless of your physical characteristics, language, sexuality, religion, or nationality, you need to demonstrate that you are willing to fit in. Yes, you want to stand out from the herd, but you don't want to be so different that you can't be trusted. This is why what you wear is so important. Sure, Steve Jobs wore jeans and a T-shirt, but he created his own empire, so he didn't have to interview for a job. Business attire is a specific uniform or even armor. It may be boring, and you may hate ties and suits or skirts and high heels, but dressing appropriately is one way of showing that while you are different enough to steer the company in a new direction, you won't rock the boat. But be true to yourself. Don't try so hard to follow the rules that you lose sight of who you are and what makes you special.

Be Polite

Politeness is really important and so is having good manners. They are both essential in the office and the boardroom, especially when dealing with clients. But they are different. Manners, or etiquette, involve a defined structure for behavior, while politeness is about respect and self-confidence. Manners are about not messing up, not embarrassing yourself or your company, and showing that you know the rules well enough to be accepted in a certain class or "club."

Politeness is about respect and it's about self-confidence. There is a trope of powerful people being rude because they can. But powerful people who are polite are so much more impressive. So as a general rule, be polite. Being either very polite or very rude can make you stand out from the herd, but being very rude is not really a viable strategy. So play it safe. Always be polite—to your boss, your kids, your neighbors, the homeless person on the street, the cashier in the supermarket, and the celeb you bump into at your local coffee shop. You can't go wrong.

YOU DON'T HAVE TO DO IT ALONE

It's a minefield out there, so you'll be relieved to know that you don't have to navigate it alone. Doing it alone might work for the hero in old-time Western movies but not for aspiring executives. Collaborating with others is a key skill you need to demonstrate. Relying on other people isn't a weakness, it's a strength.

Create Networks and Support Systems

There is no denying that much business gets done on the golf course, in executive suites of sports stadiums, during coffee breaks at conferences, and over a few drinks. Networking is everything, so take every opportunity to add people to your network. If you meet someone at an event, make a point of engaging deliberately for at least a minute or two, take their details, and follow up. Send them an email thanking them for their time, invite them to connect on LinkedIn, and then engage regularly. Comment intelligently on their posts when it's appropriate rather than just a simple "like." You'll know you've got it right if people comment on or like your comment.

Create support systems within and around your organization. Get to know the people who make things happen—the cleaners, the receptionists, the line managers. If your office is in a big building, get to know the security people at the entrance. Make friends with the barista at the nearest coffee shop: smile, chat briefly, and always tip. Maybe one day you'll need them. And if you don't, perhaps they will need you, and that favor can contribute to a positive cycle of mutual support.

Get a Brand Manager

It may sound strange, but if you want to get ahead in the corporate world, you need to become memorable by focusing on your personal brand. Think of yourself as a product and position yourself in the job market. This differs from traditional product branding in that it is more subtle. It's a matter of emphasizing your strengths, so for example, you become known as the go-to person for creating fantastic budgets or people may call you the ideas guru. A brand manager will guide you in writing op-eds for influential newspapers and associations, creating thought documents, and visibly creating value.

Get a Coach

A coach provides you with an objective perspective so you can understand your insights. Nobody expects a tennis player to reach Wimbledon without a coach, and managing a multinational company needs at least as much guidance. So why would we expect executives to manage on their own? Most importantly, a coach can guide you through a cognitive reshaping and help you create a disciplined mindset so you can discover your potential, develop it in a very thoughtful, intentional way to align with your goals, and then ultimately display your superpower in service of yourself, your organization, and your community.

IJ FINDS HIS FIT BY STANDING OUT

IJ is a clinical doctor who has spent several years honing his craft and elevating as a clinical practicing physician. When we met, he was the chief medical officer and senior vice president in charge of patient safety and quality for a large multinational multidepartment retail store.

But it soon turned out to be a nightmare. He was hoping that he'd be able to use his position to positively impact the lives of millions of patients and customers. Instead, he discovered that he was expected to play more of a marketing role than a clinical one. He was also asked to start developing programs that weren't rooted in the science of medicine but were focused on increasing market share, regardless of clinical efficacy. To add potential injury to insult, he was then asked to relocate to Bentonville, Arkansas. He had always lived on the East Coast, and he and his family were happily rooted in their Boston neighborhood. A move to Arkansas would have been a hardship posting.

That was, for him, a pivot point. He needed to get back to serving himself and his community as a clinician, and he was determined to not uproot his family.

Together, we did an in-depth assessment of his situation and worked out that there was an unbridgeable disconnect between the company's requirements and his wants and needs. It was clear to him that he did not want to remain in that position in that company. He had to find a position where he could utilize his skills and talents, and where his abilities would create a better outcome for him, his family, and the greater community.

He was already a highly visible senior executive in the healthcare industry, but we needed to make him shine. We created a roadmap for him to elevate his profile so that he would be at the forefront for any recruiters or HR managers looking for someone in his field. We established him as a thought leader through insightful articles on LinkedIn, arranged interviews with top health and technology media outlets, and shared his insights and experiences through a dedicated podcast series. We also enhanced his brand portfolio by strategically leveraging a network of professional advisors and consultants. Through collaboration with experts in the health and technology industries, we established a robust advisor network, and his partnership with the American Medical Technology Coalition helped to drive thought leadership and innovation. I encouraged him to accept a position on the board of the National Kidney Foundation where he provides expert advice.

That's a lot of work and it took a lot of time, but it was worth it. It wasn't long before he was headhunted by a recruitment firm to be the chief clinical officer and senior vice president for United Health Group, which is more aligned with his needs and wants. He needs to use his skills and expertise to make a positive contribution to patients in a range of different circumstances and he wants to continue living in the community where he and his family are happy. He has achieved both.

Stand up to stand out.

Chapter 8

RISE AND SHINE

A light on a hill cannot be hidden.
—Matthew 5:14

As we discussed in chapter 5, while the C-suite is your destination, it's not the end of the journey. Attaining the level of executive management does not mean you can coast. In fact, it's the opposite. It means that any dreams you may have had of coasting are over. It's when you settle yourself in the corner office that the work really starts, because as has been noted in influential texts for centuries, most recently and most notably in the film *Spider-Man*, "With great power comes great responsibility."

How are you going to use yours?

FEARLESS FAWN REWRITES HISTORY

Despite dropping out of school at 15 years old and ending up homeless, Fawn Weaver created a successful PR company before she was 20. But that was just the beginning. It was the success of that company, FEW Entertainment, that gave her the financial ability to take the most important step of her life—buying a farm in Kentucky. Not just any farm, though, it was the farm on which Jack Daniels and Uncle Nearest grew up.

It was all inspired by a photograph she saw in *Time* magazine of Jack Daniels next to a Black man, a slave. This man was "Uncle" Nearest Green, the master distiller who taught Jack Daniels his craft and who introduced charcoal filtering to the, until then, rather rough-and-ready Kentucky whiskey industry. The rest, as they say, is history. However, history is written by the victors, and the victors in the game of corporate America were then, and still are, white men.

So when Fawn and her husband, Keith, bought that farm and turned it into a distillery, they rewrote the history of Jack Daniels—literally—and also the future history of corporate America. Motivated by that photograph, Fawn decided to find out more, and she started researching the Jack Daniels story. Contrary to what had been believed until then, she found that Jack Daniels and Nearest Green did not relate as master and slave but as cooperative creators, as mentee and mentor, respectively.

Fast forward a few years, Nearest Whiskey is the fastest growing whiskey brand in America and is the only major distillery owned by a woman of color. Or by a woman. Or by a person of color. And that's not something Fawn takes lightly. She sees this as an enormous responsibility, because until now, very few African Americans have been able to benefit from inherited wealth in the way that successful (almost exclusively White) Americans have for generations.

Fawn's superpower and success have created a legacy that all Americans, and all African Americans, can be proud of. She's taken a story that had been presented as an example of White exploitation and turned it into one of cooperation, light, and pride, which gives us all hope.

The best whiskey is the nearest whiskey.

RISE AND SHINE

So as you ascend to the top floor, be prepared to rise and shine—to foster new ways of thinking, new ways of doing business, and new ways of relating to your shareholders, your suppliers, your staff, your customers, and all other stakeholders. The days of impersonal corporate dominance are over. It's time to stand up, to rise to the challenge.

Rise...

You've made it to the C-suite. Great. Congratulations. Now what? This is not the time to rest on your laurels; it's time to embrace your superpower with both arms and show what you're made of. So first, show up. Regardless. Show up especially on days that promise to be challenging. Granted, you may not always succeed as you had hoped, but even apparent failure need not be total failure if you learn from it. You can fail forward and fail upward if you trust the process and learn from your failures. But whatever you do, do it to the very best of your ability because it's time to shine.

...and Shine

One of the biggest advantages of executive management is that you can genuinely make an impact. You can help your business grow, integrate with the communities around you, create sustainable supply chains, and create a community of loyal customers. Don't hide your light under a bushel. Be proud of your achievements, but remember that there is a big difference between pride and conceit. Appreciate the chances you've had and celebrate your success. Give back, share the love, and help to smooth the path so others can follow. One person who's done this with aplomb is Chuck Henderson.

CHUCK CHARMS THE DONORS

Unlike other case studies in this book, there is no need to anonymize my client Charles "Chuck" Henderson, who has done such a good job of rising and shining. He is larger than life, and he shines a light that just will not be hidden under a bushel.

Chuck has used his superpower to enhance the profile of the American Diabetes Association, find new donors, significantly increase income, and effectively help to reduce the incidence of diabetes in America. A former college athlete and professional basketball player, he was appointed Chief Development Officer for the American Diabetes Association (ADA) in 2020.

He was responsible for bringing in donations, grants, funding, and partnerships to the tune of millions of dollars so that the ADA would be able to continue to work towards eradicating diabetes worldwide. To do this, he needed to shine, to elevate his own profile and that of the ADA. Chuck is very likable and charismatic, and he works well with people from all walks of life. So while doing the nitty gritty of reducing complex concepts into workable scenarios, he was finding and approaching new donors and maintaining a positive relationship with existing ones. He did this so well that he was promoted to CEO after only three years, which is when he turned to me to help him shine even brighter.

We worked together to harness the discipline and dedication he'd applied to sports and redirect them into the business world. He was able to take his natural talent and develop it into a superpower that enables him to perform at the highest level. We worked hard to make him stand out—to make it clear that he was different from the previous CEOs and that the organization was about to elevate. He was the first African American leader of the ADA, and he was one of only a few African American leaders of large organizations. Through concerted effort and concentrated media coverage, he was able to rebrand the ADA from a stuffy old medical institution into a funky public benefit organization that does good work, saves lives, and educates people about lifestyle diseases.

Under his leadership, the ADA's income increased by 475%, from $13.65M to $78.5M, between 2022 and 2024. Over the same period, he turned a $40M deficit into $116M in positive net income, with 306 days cash on hand, and increased unrestricted cash and investments from $10M to $113M, ensuring long-term financial stability. The ADA's Charity Navigator score elevated from two stars to four stars, the highest possible rating, and its mission percentage rose from 70% to 78%, surpassing BBB Wise Giving Alliance standards. In addition to that, he initiated the rollout of a 3-year strategic plan to grow organizational revenue from $131M to $500M in

10 years, created the Office of Health Equity, and launched the Obesity Association to address systemic care gaps.

Chuck's approach graphically illustrates that while the C-suite is the desired destination, it is most definitely part of the journey. He is not resting on his laurels, feeding the freshest, greenest leaves on the wreath to the cute, cuddly dragon of complacency. He has embraced his superpower, shown up, and trusted the process. He's made a positive impact on the ADA, his team, his community, and every single American who may have been headed towards diabetes. He's making a difference by helping to decrease the incidence of disease and working towards creating a healthier, happier population.

His light, which is admittedly a bright one, has not been hidden under a bushel but rather displayed for all the world to see—and to see by. Most importantly, he is sharing the love, sharing the path, and giving back.

The top floor is not the last stop, it's the platform from which you can soar. Spread your wings.

WHO ARE YOU *NOW*?

Examine your excellence to assess your progress.

You started the book by assessing who you are, in much the same way that I start with every new client. So look back to the beginning of your journal, and see who you were when you started this journey.

You've done some serious introspection, assessed your potential, and discovered, developed, and displayed your superpower. You may not see the results right away, but this process will create a lasting impact in your life that will enable you to serve others. You have taken the first step in changing your life—for good. Now you need to make it a habit.

RESOLUTION VS. REVOLUTION

We've all woken up at the end of the year and realized we haven't achieved our goals, so—before the ball drops, and we swig away at a glass of bubbly—we quickly promise ourselves we'll do it "next year." But what are the chances that we will do it next year? The same resolution! I've thought about this a lot and discovered that New Year's resolutions are not a universal thing. In fact, many other cultures do exactly the opposite. Before the Chinese New Year, for example, people pay off all their debts, resolve disputes with friends, family, and colleagues, and take care of any unfinished business. They clean their homes, and dispose of any unnecessary clutter, so that they can go into the new year with no unnecessary baggage.

I advise my clients to do something similar, which I call the New *Yours* Revolution. It's not something you do once a year, squeezing it in between getting drunk and kissing strangers; it's a lifelong evolution—a revolution. It's the continuation of the journey you're on because—as I've said before and will probably say many more times—the journey *is* the destination.

SO WHO ARE YOU *NOW*?

That is the question you need to ask yourself every day of your life. The answer will be the same but also different every day. While your core remains constant, being open to change and willing to grow means that you are a slightly different person every day, and the best part is you get to choose. You can choose what to leave behind, what to carry with you, and what new things to pick up, every day of your life.

So…who are you *now*? Today?

MAKE IT HAPPEN

I've loved writing this book, and I hope that it helps you find your superpower and helps you reach your inevitable outcome. But a book can only go so far and can't speak directly to your specific challenges and goals. This is why I offer one-on-one coaching and team workshops for individuals and companies who want to dig deeper into the Discover, Develop, Display process. These personalized interactions give me the opportunity to tailor the content and structure to each person I work with and to respond quickly and agilely as their needs evolve.

I am also available for inspirational speaking engagements countrywide. Please contact me if you would like to chat further.

- rthames@InspiritInstitute.com
- +1 410 718 8817
- www.InspiritInstitute.com
- www.linkedin.com/in/RandallThames
- www.facebook.com/Inspirit4U
- https://www.instagram.com/InspiritInstitute/#

Thank you so much for sharing the journey of this book with me. The world needs you and your superpower. I can't wait to see you shine.

–Randall

See the moment, honor the moment, master the moment, and rise to the moment.

ABOUT THE AUTHOR

Rev. Randall Ian Thames, MCC

Rev. Randall Ian Thames is a distinguished executive coach, national speaker, and spiritual leader whose life reflects a powerful blend of corporate excellence, athletic discipline, and pastoral care. Born and raised in Greater Harrisburg, Pennsylvania and a graduate of the University of Pittsburgh, he has spent over 35 years in leadership roles at renowned organizations including 3M Corporation, Johnson & Johnson, the Baltimore Orioles, Aon, and Korn Ferry.

He is the Founder, CEO, and Managing Partner of the **Inspirit Institute**, where he serves as a concierge coach to CEOs, executives, board members, physicians, and elite performers in athletics and entertainment. His coaching philosophy centers on purpose and impact. His **Discover Develop Display Your Best**™ format has been a hallmark for effective personal, professional and organizational transformation.

Rev. Thames also serves as **Deputy Pastor** at Celebration Church Columbia and Peoples Community Church Harrisburg, and is an **adjunct faculty member** at Johns Hopkins Carey Business School. He sits on several boards, including the **Kappa Alpha Psi Foundation**, where he is a life member.

A former personal fitness trainer and accomplished athlete, he has completed multiple marathons, triathlons, and obstacle course races. He lives in Howard County, Maryland with his wife of over 30 years, Trina. Together, they raised two daughters, Maya and Macy, and founded the **Inspire U Foundation**, which embodies their family mantra: **"Inspire to ignite people and organizations to their purpose, creating impact that leads to Inevitable Outcomes™."**

www.ingramcontent.com/pod-product-compliance
Lightning Source LLC
Chambersburg PA
CBHW071659210326
41597CB00017B/2250